FIGHTING FINISH

THE VOLVO OCEAN RACE

ROUND THE WORLD 2001–2002

GARY JOBSON

nomad press
a division of nomad communications

Amer Sports One *heads toward Cape Town for the finish of leg one of the Volvo Ocean Race.*

For Ted Turner
The greatest leader I have raced with.
—GJ

Nomad Press
A division of Nomad Communications

10 9 8 7 6 5 4 3 2 1
Copyright © 2002 Nomad Communications

Printed and bound in Italy.

ISBN 0-9659258-7-0

Questions regarding the ordering of this book should be addressed to:
Nomad Press
PO Box 875
Norwich, VT 05055
www.nomadpress.net
info@nomadpress.net

Contents

The fleet starts on the fourth leg of the Volvo Ocean Race—Auckland to Rio de Janeiro.

EF Language *skipper, Paul Cayard of the United States, leaps into Auckland, New Zealand, during the 1997–98 Whitbread Round The World Race. He won the seventh Whitbread and the Volvo Trophy.*

Fighting Finish
Foreword

Winning at anything requires extraordinary commitment. Often the winner is the one who can dig the deepest and summon the will and courage to fight on when others simply can't. Winning sometimes requires doing the unimaginable.

The Volvo Ocean Race demands this of all competitors. Otherwise you don't survive.

More than in any other competition in my life, my core qualities were tested during the 1997–98 Whitbread Round The World Race. At times I had to see beyond the race and make decisions for the safety of my crew. I had to see that their faith in my judgment was blind, and, if not me, then who would make the right decision in the most dangerous situations? And still, I made mistakes as I was learning to differentiate between racing and surviving. Understanding the confluence of those two concepts is key to surviving and eventually winning the Volvo Ocean Race.

The race itself gave me the richest experience I have had from sport. I had won world championships before but circumnavigating the planet we live on in the vehicle of my professional career—a sailboat—is a lifetime achievement that very few people ever have the opportunity to accomplish. The most challenging and rewarding sailing I have ever done was in the Southern Ocean. Halfway between New Zealand and Cape Horn is the most desolate, savage place on the planet. Thirty-foot waves and 35 knots of wind in 2-degree water with snowstorms and icebergs is the norm. Land-based rescue is not an option. It was then that I realized that we who sail down there are blessed because it is not Paris, Los Angeles, or St. Tropez that are the most coveted places on earth, but rather these isolated places. Living on the edge is part of what makes an experience exceptional.

If you really want to learn about yourself and test your determination to succeed, then you need to race in the most challenging conditions in the world, the Volvo Ocean Race.

—Paul Cayard
San Francisco, California

*Peter Blake wins the fifth Whitbread
Round The World Race in 1990
as Skipper of* Steinlager 2.

Dedication
to
Sir Peter Blake

The impact that Peter Blake made on round-the-world racing may never be matched, since he began at the beginning, when it was as much an adventure as a sporting challenge. Perhaps it was the combination of the two that appealed to the young, tall, blond-haired New Zealander, who had gone to England to further his career as a professional sailor.

Blake had made his mark in the lesser arenas, on the east coast of England and on the RORC circuit, including a Fastnet Race in a 35 footer, before joining Les Williams to race the 80-foot *Burton Cutter* in the inaugural Whitbread Round The World Race. His hopes, after a first-leg victory, were shattered when the aluminum hull of the boat began to break up south of the Cape of Good Hope. After repairs the boat was sailed to Rio de Janeiro to race in the last leg to Portsmouth.

It seemed that Blake's chances were doomed when his choice for the second Whitbread Race 4 years later evaporated in shards of carbon fibre when the experimental mast of *Heath's Condor* tumbled to the deck on the first leg. But when that same boat arrived first into Blake's home port of Auckland, he determined that he would skipper an all-Kiwi boat in the next race.

With the Bruce Farr–designed *Ceramco New Zealand*, Blake had the tool that he wanted with a hand-picked crew, which was as much about those who were rejected as those chosen. Still the fates turned against him in that third race. A dismasting in the Atlantic, close to where *Heath's Condor's* had failed four years earlier, ended his dream of overall victory, although he did claim two of the remaining three legs on corrected time.

Turning to Ron Holland for his next boat, *Lion New Zealand*, Blake finished second overall in the fourth race, but this simply wasn't good enough for the determined perfectionist. In 1989, he overcame a disastrous building fault, scrapped the first hull, and produced the ultimate in maxi-rating ketches, the 83-foot *Steinlager 2*, another Farr Yacht Design creation.

With *"Big Red,"* as the boat became known, Blake was able to achieve the ambition that had reached obsessive proportions in the most definitive manner possible. He won every one of the six legs. Game, set, and match!

This consummate victory allowed Peter to turn his outstanding man-management talent to other campaigns and it wasn't long before he was successful, even though the events he chose were the very pinnacles of the sport of sailing. Not for him the mundane, but only the ultimately challenging.

First it was the Trophee Jules Verne. The mark was already under 80 days, but Blake and his co-skipper, Robin Knox-Johnston (friends since they raced together on *Heath's Condor*), smashed the record with the catamaran *ENZA*.

This left only one mountain to scale—the America's Cup—and Blakey had been drawn to the sailors' Holy Grail by Sir Michael Fay. When Fay gave up, the Kiwi's mantle fell on Blake's shoulders, even to the extent of personal sacrifice to fund the entry fee when no other support seemed to materialize.

He not only won the Cup, but organized a successful defense, then began a new phase in his career, protecting the environment that he held dear. He led expeditions to the Antarctic, and had begun his reconnaissance for the improvement of the Amazon when he was tragically slaughtered by bandits.

Blake was a sailors' sailor, happiest in the elements he chose to challenge, and a force respected by everyone, particularly those against whom he had raced.

—Bob Fisher
Lymington, England

Why Volvo Ocean Race?

When the opportunity arose to acquire the famous Whitbread Round The World Race, Volvo seized the chance to become the trophy sponsor for the 1997–98 race, subsequently taking over the ownership and management of the event in June 1998.

Volvo had been looking at the sport of sailing with a view to sponsoring a major race, and the Whitbread stood for the same values that the Volvo trademark wanted to represent: adventure, excitement, and environmental awareness. Renamed the Volvo Ocean Race, the event would enable Volvo to encourage the sailing community with its sponsorship, as well as communicate to the public at large that the Volvo trademark also stood for those values. The newest generation of Volvo cars are designed to be exciting and fun to drive, of good design and environmentally friendly. The fit between this round-the-world sailing race and Volvo's car products was there.

For Volvo's other products, including trucks, buses, construction equipment, marine engines, and aero-nautical and logistic businesses, the race presented unique business-to-business opportunities at the exciting ports that the race visited around the world.

The fantastic media attention the Volvo Ocean Race received clearly demonstrated that the race reached a much wider audience than just the sailing community, and confirmed that the Volvo Ocean Race was a great communication tool for the teams, sponsors, and of course Volvo.

The Volvo Ocean Race is an adventure of epic proportions. Satellite communications brought unprecedented pictures and e-mails from all the boats to tell the story as it unfolded, as it has never been told before. *Fighting Finish: The Volvo Ocean Race, Round the World 2001–2002* is our official presentation of the race. With dramatic photography and behind-the-scenes quotes from the participants, you'll feel like you were there!

Enjoy!

—Helge Alten
Chief Executive

The Waterford Crystal Trophy Fighting Finish is awarded to the winner of the Volvo Ocean Race 2001–2002. This book takes its name from the Trophy.

Part One
The New Millennium

Fighting Finish
The New Millennium

The highlight of the (round the world) race was one particular night on the fifth leg in the Southern Ocean.
The boat was ripping along at 25 knots. We are totally under control. It dawned on me that we are perfectly
comfortable here. I realized that this was our biggest accomplishment.
Bigger than winning the whole race was to be at home in the Southern Ocean.

Paul Cayard, winner of the 1997–98 Whitbread Round The World Race for the Volvo Trophy aboard EF Language

Fighting Finish
The New Millennium

At the conclusion of a sporting event there is little mystery why one team was victorious. Early planning, individual sacrifice for the good of the team, the ability to overcome adversity, resourcefulness, maintaining a fast but steady pace, and blending the skills of many—management, sponsors, players (sailors), and design engineers—are among the attributes listed for a champion in any sport.

Most competitions last a few minutes or hours, but the Volvo Ocean Race is unique, a marathon at sea that takes at least a year to prepare for and 9 months to complete.

Over 136 days of racing on the water and covering 32,700 miles, the eight teams fight for an edge every second. They push sail bags farther outboard on deck, searching for that vital speed component, an increase in stability. The afterguards analyze and reanalyze a mosaic of weather quandaries in an attempt to outwit the competition. "What can I do to make my boat sail faster?" is each sailor's mantra. The quest keeps crews awake for extended hours, inspiring feats of pure heroism as they push their boats and themselves to limits never before achieved.

Imagine racing through ice fields at speeds 50 percent faster than the *Titanic* when she hit an iceberg

and sank. The essence of the Volvo Ocean Race is the experience of sailing on a wild sleigh ride through tunnels of bow waves that are unique to the Southern Ocean. These record-breaking passages have been the lure of this race and the reason sailors return. But when seasoned veterans like Ross Field, Gunnar

Krantz, and Marcel van Triest were horrified by speeding through minefields of ice, it makes you wonder about the sanity of their relentless pursuit.

It is the goal of reaching the finish line first that makes these intrepid competitors push so hard. In the past, the round-the-world racer's success in the Southern Ocean was knowing when to throttle back to avoid calamities. But for this edition the throttle was kept wide open.

At the start of each leg the Volvo Ocean Race fleet fanned out as each boat sought the best wind and the best route. But as the fleet converged during the final sprint to the finish, the ending was always in question. My measure of good racing is frequent lead changes. Seven of the eight boats had a podium finish on at least one leg of the race.

Historically, long-distance sailors have plied their trade far from shore and away from spectators. The Volvo Ocean Race changed all that. Competitors could tell us in their own words, several times a day, what they were thinking and how they were feeling. Those of us on shore learned first hand what it was like to compete at this level. On leg three, soon after passing Sydney's headlands, the fleet encountered a tornado. The pictures recorded on video were dra-

A stiff breeze waits for the fleet as Volvo flags waved proudly over Cape Town harbor before the start of leg two.

matic and compelling, but the sailors remained calm and businesslike. At the same time they were almost thrilled to see such a sight. We witnessed the humor on board as well: the all-women's team on *Amer Sports Too* had a contest measuring the most twisted hair; on another boat one sailor talked about missing his dog more than his girlfriend. The images in this book are unforgettable—the boats pounding through big waves, the expressions on the faces ranging from exhaustion and fear, to elation. There is an endless fascination in life at sea and the Volvo Ocean Race brought us closer to the experience than ever before.

The crew of Assa Abloy *climb the rig to display the flags of the eight different countries of the crew. Friends and family see the boats off in Ocean Village, Southampton, England.* Assa Abloy *worked at having dramatic departures in each port.*

Crowds view the V.O.60s at the Auckland Viaduct Basin Village during the Auckland stopover.

While it can be lonely racing at sea, the teams were welcomed with open arms by loved ones and fans in every port. I think the modest sailors were surprised to be treated as celebrities everywhere they stopped. The land-side adventures added depth to understanding our home, planet earth.

As the fleet arrived in each new port, thousands of people were attracted to the waterfront to witness the finish, participate in the race village, meet the crews, see the boats, wish the sailors farewell, and watch the restart. Dozens of people told me they were inspired to learn to sail after experiencing the Volvo Ocean Race.

Perhaps this race connects the world in a positive and very nice way. After the catastrophic events of September 11, 2001, you could sense the outpouring of support in England for Americans. Before the boats left the dock in Southampton, 10,000 people observed a prolonged moment of silence. Later in Sydney the eight boats formed a pinwheel as each skipper dropped a wreath in the water in memory of the great round-the-world race champion, Sir Peter Blake. The Volvo Ocean Race sailors are fierce competitors, but compassionate people.

Every boat was crewed by sailors of different nationalities. *Assa Abloy*, for example, started the race with crew from eight different countries. Skippers were more concerned with people who would fit in and contribute. The brotherhood (and sisterhood) aboard each of the V.O.60s demonstrated that people of different backgrounds can work well together toward a common goal.

Mountain climbers measure their assaults on peaks by the "degree of difficulty." Racing around the world would be off the chart if such a measure were employed, and it is not just the Southern Ocean that is hard. Consider the frustration of desperately trying to find wind in the Doldrums. Six-time round-the-world race veteran, Grant Dalton (four firsts, two seconds), was captured on video pounding the chart table when his boat, *Amer Sports One*, suddenly dropped from second to sixth on leg five. Such emotional outbursts are understandable when winning is so important.

Despite some injuries such as broken bones and intestinal infections, remarkably, every sailor made it back safely and soon recovered from injury and illness. Psychologically, though, racing around the world is not so easy to put behind you.

The late Sir Peter Blake once told me it took him one full year to recover after he won aboard the mighty red ketch, *Steinlager 2*, in the 1989–90 Whitbread. Blake said his sleep patterns were out of sync and the pressure was slow to fade, even though he had won all six legs that year.

Like the endless waves the fleet sails over, the Volvo Ocean Race was an emotional roller-coaster ride. To the casual observer the Volvo Ocean Race might appear to be a boat show, but closer inspection reveals a people show. It takes inner strength to overcome fatigue,

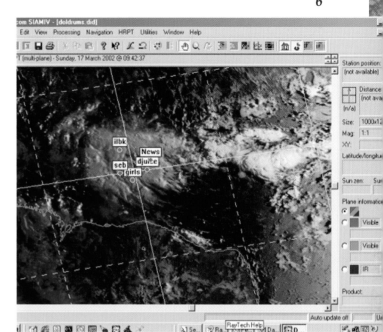

A screen grab taken by djuice *showing satellite positions of the boat. Notice the huge cloud covering the entire fleet.*

relentless weather patterns, injury, debilitating cold, and heart-pounding broaches. The key to curtailing emotional mood swings was to focus on the immediate task at hand. Worrying about the final result was a mistake. During times of stress these sailors went back to their normal routine. Again, this took discipline.

It's the leader that sets the pace. John Kostecki, skipper of *illbruck*, repeatedly told us the secret to their success was having good people. Kostecki was quietly confident throughout the race with the knowledge that his team had spent more time preparing than anyone else. This confidence was contagious.

In some sports we see defeated teams lose their spirit, but the determination of the Volvo Ocean Race sailors seemed to grow as the race progressed. With the experience of racing for weeks at a time, the crews understood how to sail their boats faster. They also learned how to sail against each other. This is why the finishes got tighter with each leg. At the end of leg eight the top five boats finished within 6 minutes 50 seconds.

Waves crashing over the helm on Amer Sports Too. *Helmsmen must face approaching waves. A hood helps but the biggest problem is salt water burning one's eyes.*

There is a tendency in sailing for the leader to get conservative down the stretch while the trailing boats get more aggressive. Kostecki understood this trend based on years of Olympic and America's Cup competition. *illbruck* never let up as the finish neared, an example that will be studied carefully by future round-the-world racers.

On every leg there was a crucial turning point that propelled one boat into the lead. There was no pattern to when this might happen. Crews had to be alert every moment, as it was easy to make a mistake and drop back; recovery was even harder. Occasionally a flier, a split with the fleet, would work out (*djuice* on leg four is a good example), but most of the time gains were made in small bites.

After nearly sinking off Cape Town on leg two, *illbruck* recovered from a 20-mile deficit by making small gains, one watch at a time. The improvement on each sked gave the crew encouragement, and the momentum propelled them into the lead by the time they arrived in Sydney.

THE VOLVO

Team SEB crew and shore crew putting new rigging in place.

In 1977 we came second to Flyer, *this despite the fact that each watch had a bottle of wine (and then some) with a dinner that came out of a well stocked freezer. We were, after all, unpaid in those days and true Corinthians. I might add that it was my error in navigation on leg three that blew our chances for first and not the wine.*

In 1981, on Alaska Eagle *we also dined large, but if the other boats were more spartan, it was a lack of interior and not the drink on board, especially if you were a French boat.*

In 1985 on Drum *things became more serious. Out went the aperitifs, and we came third to an unbeatable new Farr design.*

The Soviet entry Fazisi *in 1989 was an exceptional case, a rude machine full of vodka. We came 11th, but others in the fleet were becoming more and more professionally minded. Rumors of few books and little music aboard the front runners.*

In 1993 out went the books and music, in 1997 no changes in underwear were allowed, and in 2001 it was rumored that even talking was verboten (unless it of course had to with speed). What price success? Sharing a wet sleeping bag for a month with someone you are not particularly fond of.

Skip Novak

By contrast, *SEB*, who was leading, spent too much time looking over her shoulder as *illbruck* caught up. *SEB* probably pushed too hard with a big spinnaker in Bass Strait to keep *illbruck* back. Eventually the pressure got to *SEB* and she broached. By the time they cleared up the ensuing mess *illbruck* had claimed the lead.

With such a wide range of weather conditions the sailors had to be versatile, and able to shift gears from one pattern to the next in just minutes. At high speeds it's easy to skip from one weather pattern to the next. Weather changes can be instant and dramatic or very subtle. Anticipation is the key. A prepared crew had

the next sail and water ballast combination ready to go. Second guessing and waiting for a "confirmation" to shift gears usually resulted in being left behind.

Small boat club racers would be surprised at the non-stop trimming and adjusting that takes place on these boats.

Over the past 30 years since the first Whitbread, modern technology has improved the quality of life. Round-the-world sailors have been at the forefront of using new technology to their advantage. The list of innovations is staggering. In 1973 few could have envisioned sails built on moulds, night vision scopes, carbon fiber spars, GPS, laser range finders, gyro binoculars,

The Volvo fleet starts off Rio de Janeiro on the fifth leg of the Volvo Ocean Race to Miami. News Corp *(left) starts conservatively to avoid fouling another boat.*

electronic charts, breathable foul weather gear, bulb keels, virtual racing on the Internet, instant communications (picture, voice, and text), and qualified people to use these tools efficiently in the heat of battle.

While technology has made racing more efficient and faster, the "comfort" factor has decreased dramatically, as the quest for speed dictates the bare minimum of food, sleep, clean (or even dry) clothes, and relaxation. It is extremely difficult to get good rest when the noise below is deafening and the boat's motion is so violent. Life on board takes its toll, with some crews reported losing up to 25 pounds (11 kilos) on one leg alone.

Respect is the reward athletes earn for excellence in competition. There is no greater honor than over-coming adversity through resourcefulness and pure grit, and turnarounds are what fans love and respect. Through the nine legs of the Volvo Ocean Race there were many examples of superhuman efforts to come back after major setbacks. Each rebound, even when it was at the back of the fleet, demonstrated how determined the sailors were to win.

www.VolvoOceanRace.org

Part Two
The Teams

Assa Abloy Racing Team

Assa Abloy *ploughs through the waves at the start of leg two of the Volvo Ocean Race from Cape Town to Sydney.*

Day Seven, Leg One

*Last night's sailing reminded us all why we keep coming back in spite of all the beating and discomfort.
We were reaching along in 16 plus knots with reaching spinnaker, bright moon, warm air, dolphins chuffing
all around, and gaining bearing on our chiseling competitors. Not bad for a night shift job.*

Mark Rudiger

Assa Abloy Racing Team

After *EF Language's* winning finish in the 1997–98 Whitbread, two of *EF's* management staff, Johan Salèn and Richard Brisius, and their company, Atlant Ocean Racing, continued to oversee the elements needed to mount a successful yacht racing campaign. This included concept and design choices, the shore and boat crews, the sponsorship fulfillment programs, and the public relations staff. Atlant found sponsorship for a Volvo Ocean Race 2001–2002 entry from the Assa Abloy Group, a consortium of international companies that is the world's leading manufacturer and supplier of locks and security solutions. With businesses in or near all the ports of call, and as a company focusing on a direct, people-to-people approach, they were a natural main sponsor, and saw the race as a way to integrate their more than 100 companies worldwide.

Atlant's role was to organize their Volvo Ocean Race campaign. Richard Brisius has said that a skipper in modern times cannot do everything singlehandedly to the best outcome in a competition such as the Volvo Ocean Race.

Atlant had sold their winning *EF* campaign boats to the *illbruck Challenge* team as tune up boats. With Assa Abloy as a sponsor, they purchased *Chessie Racing's* on-the-water assets for several months of Southern Ocean training in Sydney, Australia.

Having decided to mount a two-boat campaign, they chose Farr Yacht Design as the designer for their boats, and Green Marine, in Lymington, England, as the builder. Green Marine has produced an impressive list of winning boats, including the last Louis Vuitton Cup winner, *Prada*. Typical of Atlant's thoroughness, Jason Carrington, the first *Assa Abloy* crew member hired, had apprenticed at Green Marine, and was *Assa Abloy's* construction manager, with the understanding that he would later sail on the boat as bowman.

The boats were built on a female mould, not the usual male mould, as this was thought a more efficient way to produce two exact boats. Thus, the distinctively gleaming golden yellow-ochre color of the Kevlar cloth could be seen through the clear outer layer of lacquer. *Assa Abloy's* graphics were so well-designed that they were entered in the 2001 International Art Direction and Design Award Contest in London.

Securing the services of veteran Magnus Olsson set the guiding tone for this team. Olsson had sailed in four round-the-world races, and was helmsman aboard *EF Language* for their 1997–98 win. The

Neal McDonald of the United Kingdom, skipper of Assa Abloy, *displays the trophy for winning the Sydney Hobart Race of leg three. McDonald already seems to be thinking ahead.*

Day Four, Leg Five

Yes it's hot, hot, hot, hot!
Burned my feet on the deck going up
to check a rainsquall.

Mark Rudiger

The wind has a snow fence effect along the hills of Rio de Janeiro. If she gets too close, Assa Abloy *will run out of wind.*

Stu Wilson, like many other crew members, spent count-less hours repairing sails below deck. The V.O.60s carried their own sewing machines.

irrepressible Olsson is always smiling, always posi-tive, always cheerful. And always seriously intent on winning. Roy Heiner, hired as skipper, said of Olsson before the start in Southampton, "He is coach, he is father. He's a fantastic helmsman. A fantastic yachtsman. Always happy. Always looking at the positive side."

Mark Rudiger, another *EF* alumnus, signed on as navigator, adding to an international crew that was assembled from ocean race veterans and maxi sailors. In Southampton, he said, "We know we've got a good boat. We've got a great team."

J/22 and J/24 world champion Chris Larson joined the boat for leg three. Larson is a boatspeed and tacti-cal specialist. In spite of a slow start in Sydney, he helped turn the fortunes of *Assa Abloy* around as they won leg three. This was a syndicate of experienced, dedicated sailors, supported by an equally dedicated managerial and public relations staff.

After a disappointing leg one, management decid-ed to replace skipper Roy Heiner with Neal McDonald of Great Britain. If the McDonald name sounds familiar, it's because Neal's wife, Lisa, was the skipper of the all-women's team *Amer Sport Too*.

These races aren't over until the end. And pushing right until the end is something that I really intend to do. Not just on individual legs but on the whole race. It is amazing what can happen. You can lose a lot of ground. You can gain a lot of ground. But if you keep pushing hard you're obviously going to improve you chances.

Neal McDonald

The view from the spinnaker pole is spectacular as Assa Abloy effortlessly cuts through the water.

djuice dragons

Notice the helmsman aboard djuice leaning forward. He looks like he is literally pushing the boat to sail faster. The three crew on the rail are surely philosophical in a quiet discussion.

Day Three, Leg One

Maybe the pink banner of my friends at the start "you crazy guy" has some truth in it!

Wouter Verbraak

djuice dragons

djuice dragons evolved from *Innovation Kvaerner*, the 1997–98 Whitbread Race syndicate from Norway that finished fourth overall. With experience in this uniquely demanding sporting venture, the three principal players from the *Innovation Kvaerner* campaign joined forces once again to launch *djuice*. Skipper Knut Frostad, project manager Harald Hjort, and shore manager, BJ Grimholt, felt they had ascended the steep learning curve. They left behind the atmosphere of discord that often prevailed in the *Innovation* camp in 1997, and were dedicated to improving management and teamwork. Each crew member of *djuice* was carefully screened for motivation and attitude. Indeed, one of the few things this team retained from their 1997–98 debut was the dragon talisman, only this time, the mythical serpent changed colors from lime green to hot magenta.

djuice dragon's management made a bold design decision. Frostad figured the only way he was going to get an edge on the Farr Yacht Design boats was to race a rival design. When he got wind that New Zealand's winning America's Cup designer Laurie Davidson had a Volvo Ocean 60 in the model stage, he jumped for it. After tank testing four, one-fifth-scale models at the Woolfson facility in Southampton, England, *djuice* had

two identical boats built by Mick Cookson's yard in Auckland, New Zealand, and flown to Miami for fitting out. Meanwhile, Burns Fellow from North Sails was working with *djuice* sail manager Paul Davis, testing a

variety of sail shapes in a wind tunnel. The two boats eventually match-raced across the Atlantic to satisfy the blue-water passage rules requirement and finished just hours apart.

A former Olympian (sailboard and Flying Dutchman) with two ocean race campaigns behind him, the charismatic Frostad was the undisputed team leader of *djuice*. His crew of seven different nationalities included two-time Whitbread veteran and New Zealand America's Cup sailor Erle Williams, who was Frostad's tactician. Norwegians Espen Guttormsen and Christian "Judge" Johannessen were back for a second round-the-world duel on the ocean, and Danish Olympic Finn and Soling sailor Stig Westergaard trimmed and drove.

The *djuice* campaign began in 1999 when Frostad and Hjort conceived a commercial project around the race that they hoped would sustain itself. It included a lecture tour, a book, and a merchandising plan, as well as a sailing school for young people—all sponsored by the business community. Starting a $15 million (U.S.) business that needed to have a fully-prepared boat and crew on the starting line in just two years was a tall order. After three refusals from major sponsors they thought were ready to back

December 4, 2001. djuice off Sydney. V.O.60s at high speeds are remarkably stable.

Knut Frostad, skipper of djuice, *made a bold move selecting designer Laurie Davidson to draw the lines of his boat. Knut is noted as a deep thinker.*

them, their presentation to Djuice, Telenor Mobile's new internet company—an offspring of Norway's tele-communications giant—hit paydirt.

As for the hot magenta and black color combination, Frostad stressed the need to look different from other teams. "The 'lime army' concept worked well last time," he said. "We hope to be even more successful this time."

The djuice *crew in front of a huge iceberg they just avoided. Could the crew possibly be this happy or were they simply relieved to have dodged another iceberg?*

Wet sanding the hull is therapeutic for the shore crew and the sailors. Knowing that you spent some time sanding the bottom makes surfing that much more enjoyable.

Knut acknowledged prior to the start that he made a courageous decision to hire Laurie Davidson over Farr Yacht Design: "At the time that we were planning our project two years before the race, there were only two designers that had started working on this race and that was Laurie Davidson and Farr Yacht Design. We met with Davidson and liked what we saw. We thought he had done a really good study, and had started to work for a group that is now behind *Team New Zealand.* Then we went to Farr Yacht Design. You have to realize that get-

ting a Farr Yacht Design boat doesn't mean that you get the same boat as everyone else. We knew that *illbruck* had worked with Farr Yacht Design for a long time. If we got a faster boat than *illbruck*, and if I was John Kostecki, I wouldn't be very happy. On the other hand, Davidson convinced us that he had some great ideas and so far in testing they have proven right for making a boat easy to drive fast. It has strength in some areas that we know the Farr Yacht Design boat is weak and we believe this is going to be a good boat."

Day Six, Leg Two

Every new guy stepping on deck looks more and more weird as we wear different combinations of hats, helmets, balaclavas and goggles . . . Arve [Roaas] is very popular as he is the only guy who knows how to operate the heater.

Knut Frostad

djuice *high speed reaching in freezing conditions with* Jacques Vincent *on the helm. Note the intensity of the crew.*

Team Profile
illbruck Challenge

Baltimore after Leg Six

The Volvo Ocean Race is tough. It is mentally demanding. Yeah we don't have great food, it is cold and wet, we do not have warm showers. You're sharing a bunk. You're sharing a sleeping bag. But it is a race. Everybody else works under the same conditions and it is a tough race and very competitive. Mentally it can be a struggle at times but we have a great crew, and that winning attitude.

John Kostecki

illbruck Challenge

"Success Through Motivation, Flexibility, and Teamwork"

The motto of illbruck, the privately held international company headquartered in Munich, Germany, carried through to its entry in the Volvo Ocean Race 2001–2002, with the addition of "intense preparation" to the list of qualities held dear. This team had been at it for three long years before they heard the starting gun in Southampton. Some even suggested they might have passed their peak. But *illbruck* also had visions of two of competitive yachting's sugar plums dancing in their heads to motivate them. Skipper John Kostecki said before the start, "We're pretty anxious to get going on this race after all the training that we've done. We're ready."

Willi Illbruck, the founder of the illbruck company, began successfully campaigning his one-tonner, *Pinta*, in 1969. He sailed a variety of Pintas to victory in many grand prix regattas, including the Sardinia Cup, the Admiral's Cup, and the SORC. Meanwhile, he built illbruck into a multinational supplier of industrial and residential sealant; filtration, insulation, and bath systems; and architectural surfaces.

Son Michael Illbruck, now CEO of the company,

picked up the torch after the 1997 Admiral's Cup, and has committed illbruck to a large-scale effort to win yachting's top prizes.

The Illbruck family believes that the exposure the company receives from the efforts has proved to be a most positive benefit to the company as a whole, from global marketing to internal corporate identification.

The Illbruck stamp of thoroughness is on this intended two-pronged attack on competitive yachting's highest prizes. Michael Illbruck is fond of using the phrase ". . . and the fight goes on." He chose John Kostecki, veteran America's Cup tactician, to be his skipper for the Volvo Ocean Race, with the thought that John would then continue on as *illbruck's* America's Cup skipper.

John Kostecki is one of the world's best sailors. He broke into the international stage with a silver medal performance in the Soling Class in the 1988 Olympic Games. He has also won eight world championships in six classes.

The *illbruck Challenge* boat was built in-house at illbruck facilities in Germany, by illbruck employees under the supervision of Killian Bushe, who built *Innovation Kvaerner* for the last Whitbread Round The World Race. The Farr Yacht Design boat chosen by illbruck was extensively tested before being selected. This careful preparation is integral to the illbruck method of operation.

33,698 miles to go and the crew was hiking hard.

illbruck skipper John Kostecki at the press conference after winning leg four from Auckland to Rio de Janeiro. Kostecki gained confidence talking with the press throughout the race.

Day Seven, Leg One

'hoo' Ray (Davies) made up for taking my sleeping bag liner by putting his wet socks in my dry boots, an easy mistake to make in the dark. Life in our small world is full of excitement.

Day 16, Leg One

Ray has stopped using my boots to store his wet socks, I think because my boots are wet now.

Mark Christensen

While waiting for their boat, the *illbruck* crew secured both *EF* boats for crew training and selection. With a matched set of trial boats, they did not feel they had to build two of their own. Extensive training in Charleston, South Carolina, racing up the east coast of the United States, transatlantic passages, and the Sydney–Hobart and Fastnet races brought this well-seasoned team to the United Kingdom in August 2001 for the start. The crew, comprising an international mix of sailors, had 12 round-the-world races and considerable America's Cup experience amongst them.

John Kostecki is direct in his assessment of *illbruck*: "We have a great team. We have the best team."

When asked about the impressive *illbruck* preparation, so thorough and so extensive, he sticks to his guns: "Preparation helped, but we have all the right people and that is the secret to our success."

For Michael Illbruck, sponsoring a boat in the Volvo Ocean Race combined a love for sport and business: "First of all we have a long racing tradition in sailing. After the 1997 Admiral's Cup I basically picked it up from my Dad and we all said that we have to continue this and bring it to a different level. It is also a marketing opportunity. For us sailing has been a positive corporate image vehicle for more than 20 years. That is why we do this: to bring this race round the world to all illbruck locations. I hope it is going to fascinate our staff, our customers, and partners, and they all get excited."

illbruck on the way to her first-place finish of leg two with the Sydney Opera House in the background.

Day Six, Leg Two

Saw our second iceberg today. A hotel and a ski lift and it would have made a good resort.

Mark Christensen

Day Seven, Leg Four

Many people say that it is more dangerous crossing a busy city street than racing in the Southern Ocean. I hope they are right!

John Kostecki

illbruck set a new World Record of 484 nautical miles in 24 hours during leg seven.

Nautor Challenge

Amer Sports One
Amer Sports Too

The Nautor Challenge boats, Amer Sports One *and* Amer Sports Too, *at the start of leg five from Rio de Janeiro to Miami. The women aboard* Amer Sports Too *watch their boat's performance against stablemate* Amer Sports One. *Both boats were about to dip right-of-way* illbruck.

Day 25, Leg One

We take each mile gained as pennies from heaven. Humbleness and gratitude are probably the most important traits that an offshore yachtsman must learn. And this is only the beginning of a 9-month odyssey.

Grant Dalton

Baltimore after Leg Six

It's very rewarding when I see the performance getting better every leg.

Lisa McDonald

Nautor Challenge

When Leonardo Ferragamo of the famous Italian fashion family acquired Nautor, builders of the Swan sailboat line, he began looking for ways to increase and regain Nautor's brand recognition in the sailing market. After all, a Swan sailboat won the first Whitbread. Given that Paul Cayard was a member of Ferragamo's Board of Directors, it was suggested that Ferragamo build a Volvo Ocean 60 and sponsor a team in the Volvo Ocean Race.

Learning of Ferragamo's interest, Volvo Ocean Race Chief Executive Helge Alten traveled to Italy, where Ferragamo told Alten he was intrigued by the idea of putting the Nautor name back into the yachting spotlight, as well as globally promoting his line of high fashion products. Simultaneously, Fred Anderssen, the head of the winning EF syndicate in the 1997–98 Whitbread, was interested in mounting another successful round-the-world race campaign. Anderssen and Ferragamo went to work. They decided on a two-boat entry and recruited sporting goods equipment manufacturer Amer Sports, and the Swiss bank, UBS, as marketing partners. The internationally recognized Amer Sports company, with its associated brands (Wilson, Atomic, and Suunto), eagerly signed on as a means to achieve worldwide leadership in its global market. UBS had sponsored many yachting projects, and quickly joined this high-profile campaign.

At the same time, round-the-world champion Grant Dalton was considering doing the Volvo Ocean Race while he was working on a multihull for a French event modestly titled, The Race. Dalton went on to win The Race aboard *Club Med*. In five previous Whitbreads Dalton had finished with three firsts and two seconds.

Paul Cayard was recruited as a consultant to the project. The syndicate would build two boats by different designers. The Argentine, German "Mani" Frers, Jr., who was following in his famous father's footsteps, designed one boat. German Frers, Sr. was a long-time designer for Nautor Swan. The other design came from Farr Yacht Design.

With time passing swiftly the syndicate got in touch with Grant Dalton six months before the start. Dalton signed on.

Lisa McDonald had struck out at starting her own syndicate and welcomed Dalton's call and the request to race Nautor's second boat. Some of her talented and experienced *EF Education* shipmates joined her and an international roster of match-racing and blue-water sailors was put together. This would be the

The two Nautor Challenge boats in action just after the start. Amer Sports Too had a problem as the spinnaker ripped in half. The crew reset a new sail in just 2 minutes.

fourth time for an all-women's team in the round-the-world race, following in the traditions of *Maiden*, *Heineken*, and *EF Education*.

Dalton now faced the daunting task (as he had in 1997–98) of selecting which of two dissimilar boats he preferred to race. Nineteen days before the start, Dalton was still not sure. Finally, at the 11th hour, he picked the Frers hull.

With the boats in the water only two-and-a-half months, versus *illbruck's* 3 years, the Nautor syndicate was scrambling to be ready for the start. Dalton expected setbacks: "There is no way you can throw things on a light boat, never trial them, and not expect them to break down."

Lisa McDonald commented, "It has been an enormous amount of pressure getting these boats ready . . . having Grant as the manager and an organizer, he's actually pulled together a good group of about 50 people that have just done an outstanding job in the last 2 months."

Amer Sports One at Coromandel Penninsula. 500 pounds of extra gear on the windward rail gave the boat added stability.

McDonald wasn't surprised when Dalton chose the Frers boat, saying, "It was a tough call. And I'm glad I didn't have to make that decision . . . We've got two really good race boats here."

Amer Sports Too carried an extra crew member, 13 versus the usual 12. The Volvo Ocean Race allowed the women's team an extra person to even out crew weight. The other skippers unanimously approved the change. *Amer Sports Too* watch captain, Katie Pettibone, had mixed feelings about the change. "I can certainly see both sides of the fence but I know some of the skippers initially thought, 'Hey, you know, girls, the rule was always 12 people, it wasn't weight.' Last time around it was weight and crew num-

ber. I'm happy they changed it. I think it makes it more fair for us."

And on the subject of the helpfulness of training against a future competitor, Pettibone had this to say: "Dalton is definitely a help. He pushes us as much as he does his own crew."

McDonald was asked prior to the start if it was a special challenge developing such an international group into a crew. She replied: "We didn't have much time for trials or as many tryout periods as some of the other teams might have had. But most of us know each other and have sailed with or against each other on the international circuits, one design and match racing, so it's quite fun to pull everyone together."

Amer Sports One out in front of the other V.O.60s at the start of leg four from Auckland to Rio de Janeiro. Winning the start is always a big morale boost.

Amer Sports One skipper Grant Dalton commanded great respect from his competitors.

Amer Sports One *breaks through heavy seas in the early hours of leg eight from La Rochelle to Göteborg.*

Day 11, Leg Five

A good sked and you feel great about your possibilities to advance in the fleet. A bad sked and you look everywhere to improve boat speed. Which helmsmen should steer, how to trim, how hard to press the boat, and which sail takes you in the direction you want to go.

Roger Nilson

Day Two, Leg Three

There have been terrible bush fires near Sydney and offshore, you could smell the smoke before you got the wind shift from the land. As the day went on, the fleet raced south under smouldering skies. The end of the day brought some of the most turbulent weather I have seen for a long time. I was getting an hour's shuteye when the call came, waterspout ahead, and building. It was a huge water-funnel from the sea to the sky, fortunately not in our path but it looked as if it could cause a serious amount of damage if you got tangled up with it.

Lisa McDonald

The stack of sails on the windward rail acts as a spray shield for the crew in the cockpit.

Day Five, Leg Two

It's great, it is all worth it, as we read the speedo,
18, 18.4, 19.8, 20.2, 23 . . . fantastic . . .

Emma Westmacott

Amer Sports Too *makes her way through heavy seas in the legendary Southern Ocean.*

Amer Sports Too *skipper*
Lisa McDonald.

Considering that Dalton had completed five Whitbreads, Dalton was asked before the start if it gets easier or harder as time goes by. "Things are quite different for us in this campaign. We haven't had a lot of time. We've broken away from the mould almost taking a Frers boat instead of the traditional Farr shape. So there's quite a bit of anticipation and also concern that we've got it right and we won't know that until after the race starts."

Why did he go with the Frers boat over the Farr Yacht Design boat? "Well in the end we think it is a better package for the race. It's lighter, it seems to perform well in a breeze. It doesn't seem to have any serious downsides in light air except smooth water when its shear size slows it down. You know we didn't have to take it. It wasn't a knee-jerk reaction without preparation. We thought it was a better package for what we'll encounter over the next 9 months."

March 6, 2002. Amer Sports Too *sailing into Rio de Janeiro.*
The team looks relieved to finally reach the finish.

Team News Corp

The sails are trimmed to perfection on this close reach.

News Corp, Day Two, Leg One

Everyone aboard News Corp was stoked to be finally on our way and actually racing after such a long build up. All the guys who were saying sad goodbyes to wives and girlfriends not three hours before now had huge grins on their faces as the realization hit them that this is what we had come for and there was no more boat work, no more sail work, no more food to pack, there was only one thing to do and that was actually race.

Ably Pratt

Team News Corp

eam News Corp was impressive on paper. The crew included 1993–94 Whitbread Race winner Ross Field, who left his syndicate head office and stepped aboard into the strategist/tactician role when it was time to go sailing. He's only 52, after all. The Volvo Ocean Race 2001–2002 was his fourth round-the-world race. No doubt Field's experience came in handy for skipper Jez Fanstone, an Englishman who sailed the last race on *Silk Cut*. Nick White, the once shore-bound meteorologist who was a key factor in Field's win with *Yamaha*, was *News Corp's* navigator. Two-time America's Cup–winning navigator Peter Isler joined the team for leg three. And the rest of the rotating crew hailed from New Zealand, Australia, Ireland, and Great Britain, and read like a who's who of ocean racing.

Then there's Bart Simpson, a tough little kid any boat would be proud to have on board. Bart helped fly the colors of his cartoon family's producer/distributor, News Corporation, Rupert Murdoch's media empire. Murdoch used the race to encourage company pride and motivation, employee recognition, and team building within his multi-platform media company. Ironically, external public relations

were not a priority for this team. At one point Field mentioned the boat was going to be named after a movie but that thought was scuttled in favor of naming the boat after the corporate parent.

News Corp being lifted for a final cleaning.

Unlike many other teams that used training venues worldwide, *News Corp* established headquarters at New Zealand's Viaduct Basin, and counted on the weather vagaries of the North Island to provide the variety of training they needed. They bought the slightly used Farr Yacht Design *Merit Cup* that was not selected by Grant Dalton in the last race as a training vessel and quietly went to work.

When it came to selecting a design for their new boat, *News Corp* joined the majority of competitors and went with Farr Yacht Design. Counting the Volvo Ocean Race 2001–2002, Farr Yacht Design has now designed 21 of the 28 Whitbread and Volvo Ocean 60s that have sailed in this race since 1993–94. Seven other naval architects have designed one boat apiece. Farr Yacht Design's experience with these high-tech fliers is overwhelming. *News Corp's* potential designs were sent around the world six times by computer before tank testing began.

News Corp was shipped to New York for launching, and her subsequent transatlantic qualifying sail. Peter Isler used that event for a double first: his first sail on a Volvo Ocean 60, and his first transatlantic. He quickly got the gist of these boats. "When the

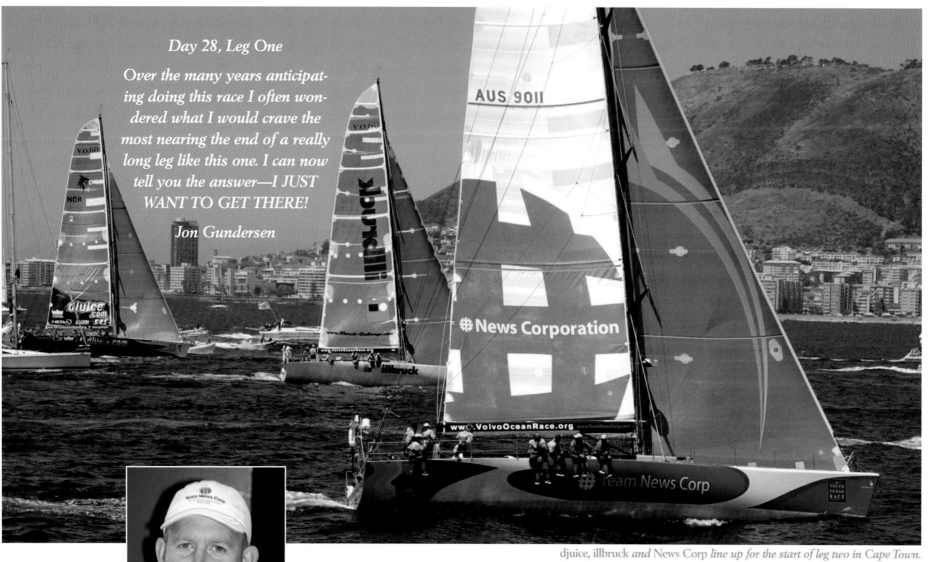

Day 28, Leg One

Over the many years anticipating doing this race I often wondered what I would crave the most nearing the end of a really long leg like this one. I can now tell you the answer—I JUST WANT TO GET THERE!

Jon Gundersen

djuice, illbruck *and* News Corp *line up for the start of leg two in Cape Town.*

Jez Fanstone, skipper of News Corp, *was a steady leader throughout the race.*

call comes to tack or jibe an intense effort begins above and below decks that involves everyone on the crew," Isler wrote afterward. "I can't begin to recount how many pounds of sails and gear I hefted from one side to the other during the trip. At times you feel more like the Mayflower moving man than a sailboat racer."

News Corp was underwritten by Rupert Murdoch's giant media company. Field traveled to New York during the Brazilian stopover to update Murdoch and his son, Lachlan, on the race. Even though *News Corp* had mixed results at that point, Murdoch seemed happy with the project. Field chuckled, "I'm sure he would have told me if he felt otherwise."

Day Seven, Leg One

If ocean racing were meant to be easy,
everyone would be out here doing it.

Ross Field

May 26, 2002. News Corp *and* illbruck *close to Ushant during leg eight from La Rochelle to Göteborg.*
News Corp *beat* illbruck *by a mere 1 minute, finishing only 4 minutes behind the winning boat.*

Ross Field

SEB ploughs through waves at the start of leg two from Cape Town to Sydney. Split wheels allow the helmsman to steer to windward, giving him greater visibility.

Day Five, Leg Six

The biggest challenge is to be able to keep the focus and the momentum and concentration and don't let yourself go down when things go bad. You just have to understand it's another day tomorrow, another hour, another boat to get and to catch. So you always have to keep the spirit high, that's the big thing. And also, of course, have a good team on board and make sure everything works out.

Gunnar Krantz

Team SEB

If there was one moment that fully motivated *SEB* skipper Gunnar Krantz and five of his crew, it was when they fell into an unaccountable hole within spitting distance of the finish in Auckland at the end of leg four during the 1997–98 Whitbread. They were in first place at the time, with what seemed like a comfortable lead. Krantz and his mates aboard *Swedish Match* could only watch helplessly as four trailing boats headed inshore to avoid the hole and passed them. At the end, that fifth place finish dropped *Swedish Match* to third overall instead of second. The memory lingered, and inspired.

For the Volvo Ocean Race 2001–2002 Krantz shipped his whole team and their two training boats (*Silk Cut* and *Toshiba* from 1997–98) to Cascais, Portugal, for 6 months of hard work in a rigorous, military atmosphere. It turned out to be one of the worst winters in Cascais history, perfect for cold, heavy-weather testing of boats, gear, and crew. "No stone has been left unturned," Krantz said when the ordeal was over. Every piece of data collected about sails and gear was considered in the design process for the team's new boat.

Krantz and five others on board were together on *Swedish Match*, including watch leaders Rodney Ardern and Tony Mutter.

SEB selected a Farr Yacht Design boat, but in the wake of the Cascais experience they brought plenty of ideas to the table. The boat's interior was modified to facilitate the movement of gear to increase stability. On deck the team opted for two main hatches instead of one on the centerline in order to make faster sail changes on the shorter legs.

The crew of *SEB* commanded respect: Collectively, there were 16 round-the-world races and approximately 500,000 ocean-racing miles among the 12 sailors. Navigator Marcel van Triest and skipper Gunnar Krantz were participating in their fourth race. Krantz was unquestionably in charge, and he had a clear vision of how his job had changed over the course of more than a decade. "It is now evident that the skipper's role is to manage a skilled crew. The days when you had one almighty God are over. The way the team is put together, the diversity of skill and personality is as important as the best possible design of sails and boat."

The veteran Krantz also understood his sponsor responsibility, which was music to the ears of the 15-company partnership backing Team SEB. "Nobody denies the fact that these Volvo projects deliver more than five times the investment," Krantz acknowl-

SEB arrives in Sydney Harbour as the second boat in the second leg from Cape Town to Sydney.

SEB *skipper Gunnar Krantz kept his cool during times of adversity.*

edged, "but the cold commercial value must be combined with other values that are more related to employees and customers."

SEB, one of the largest groups of banks and finance companies in Sweden, had a vision of being the leading electronic supplier of financial services in Europe. Gunnar Krantz had a vision of doing well enough in the 2001–2002 race to wipe out forever his memory of that windless hole off Auckland. The two visions were most compatible.

Krantz recruited an interesting combination of some experienced people like Dutch navigator Marcel van Triest with some newcomers. His rationale: "We will always need new blood in this sport. If not it will arrest the development of the sport. We need enthusiasm. We need good, solid sailors. When the weather is tricky or driving is very, very tough you need experience mixed in with the new enthusiasm on board." Krantz was the big brother of the team. His cool demeanor came in handy throughout the race as the team faced several major setbacks, including a broken mast and snapped rudder.

Krantz's leadership style reflected his hard-driving focus, especially during the transitions from long to short legs. "You have to be able to click in a different gear. It is a thing you have to prepare before you start the leg or before you start the race. To think through all these differences so you understand what is involved. Especially the fourth leg, when you have the Southern Ocean section coming around Cape Horn and then another gear through the Tropics."

Krantz's attitude was consistently upbeat; when asked if he and his crew enjoyed themselves, he replied: "We had fun. It's a very privileged way of living as well as competing."

Icebergs close astern to SEB. The most dangerous icebergs were bergy bits and growlers, which lurked on or just below the surface. The tension of sailing through the maze of ice is evident.

Today it is a race on land as much as it is on water because if you don't give back to the sponsors what they've invested for, you don't have a job next time. So it is not just focusing on the race and the points and beating the other opponents, you also have to be focused on being a professional yachtsman in terms of an ambassador for your partners in the project. Much bigger pressure on the guys in the projects these days.

Gunnar Krantz

SEB would be keen to improve her standing on this leg. The graphic on the foot of the jib seems to match the bow wave.

Team Tyco

In heavy winds like this, does the crew think about the broken rudder on the previous leg?

Day Nine, Leg Three

We all signed up to do the Volvo Ocean Race and agreed that we would be looking forward to some close racing, but this is some of the tightest racing we have ever experienced.

Steve Hayles

Team Tyco

*T*eam *Tyco* was named for American Dennis Kozlowski's sponsoring company, Bermuda-based Tyco International, Ltd. With telecommunications, electronics, fire and security, health care, and capital divisions, Tyco had a presence in over 100 countries. Kozlowski was a passionate sailor, having purchased the beautifully restored J-boat *Endeavour*. Tyco was also a substantial sponsor of Team Dennis Conner's America's Cup challenge. Kozlowski viewed the Volvo Ocean Race as a way to promote global brand recognition for Tyco's diverse businesses, as well to affirm his appreciation for the accomplishment and romance of boats and the water.

Team Tyco's syndicate manager, Australian Mike Castania, had been Kozlowski's long-time sailing companion and boat captain, and together they envisioned a syndicate sponsorship for the Volvo Ocean Race. Castania's first move was to interview several candidates for the skipper position, and he signed veteran round-the-world racer Kevin Shoebridge of New Zealand for the job. Shoebridge fitted in perfectly with Kozlowski's and Castania's belief that a team approach to the project would be most beneficial, and give the syndicate the best chance of doing well.

This was Shoebridge's fifth round-the-world race. In his four previous circumnavigations he was on boats that finished first twice (1989–90, *Steinlager 2*; 1993–94, *New Zealand Endeavour*), and second twice (1985–86, *Lion New Zealand*; 1997–98, *Merit Cup*). The Volvo Ocean Race 2001–2002 was his first as

skipper, and Shoebridge considered the transition from crew to captain as "not really a step into the unknown, but a step up. I've been lucky enough to have done a lot of sailing with (Sir Peter) Blake and (Grant) Dalton and watch their campaigns, and also tried to glean everything I could from the *Team New Zealand* campaigns and bring it all together."

Shoebridge selected a crew deep with experience. Ten of the 12 crew had previous round-the-world race experience. Even so, Shoebridge plugged experts in along the way, "to bring in more technical help on some of the shorter legs," including Richard Dobbs, America's Cup veteran. Dobbs blended *Tyco's* strategy and weather information at the same time.

Tyco's single boat was built using balsa core technology at premier boatbuilder Eric Goetz' yard in Middletown, Rhode Island. The balsa core was a departure from the more usual PVC foam core construction. Completed early, the boat was thoroughly tested against *illbruck* and *News Corp* in the 2000 Sydney–Hobart race, and then across both the Tasman Sea and in transatlantic passages.

The sail program aboard *Tyco* was overseen by Grant "Fuzz" Spanhake, a three-time crewman on the round-the-world race, a four-time America's Cup

Tyco arrives in Cape Town to finish fourth on the first leg.

Tyco in the Parade of Sail in Auckland. The New Zealand sailors were mighty proud to be in their home waters.

Tyco skipper, Kevin Shoebridge.

campaign participant, and a well-respected sail designer. Spanhake joined the crew starting with leg six. American Mike Toppa, who was on board *Chessie Racing* for several legs in 1997–98, also had input into the sail program.

Team Tyco entered the Volvo Ocean Race well-prepared and well-funded and, unusually for modern times, singularly sponsored. Kozlowski, the sponsor-ing company's then CEO, in league with Castania, set out to find a boat design (Farr Yacht Design), have it built, and find a compatible and competitive crew under the able leadership of a seasoned skipper. In assessing their chances pre-start, Shoebridge was modest: "I think this is really a talented fleet. It's going to be really close racing . . . it's going to be a tightly fought battle to the end."

Leg Four

Please take note that when we start talking about coming back down here in four years time that we should be locked away until we come to our senses.

Steve Hayles

The trimmers kept their weight to windward as Tyco surfed in the Southern Ocean during leg four. When sailors have their hoods up on a downwind leg, you know it's cold.

Leg One: **Southampton to Cape Town**

Leg Two: **Cape Town to Sydney**

Leg Three: **Sydney to Auckland**

Leg Four: **Auckland to Rio de Janeiro**

Leg Five: **Rio de Janeiro to Miami**

Leg Six: **Miami to Baltimore**

Leg Seven: **Annapolis to La Rochelle**

Leg Eight: **La Rochelle to Göteborg**

Leg Nine: **Göteborg to Kiel**

Only Assa Abloy and Amer Sports Too started cleanly off Miami. The other six boats had to scramble to return and restart properly.

Part Three

The Volvo Ocean Race
Round the World 2001–2002

Leg One
Southampton to Cape Town

Rough weather is encountered as djuice heads into the Atlantic off Portugal. The helmsman keeps his hood down to sense the wind.

Assa Abloy, Day 14

WE'RE FREE, WE'RE FREE!!

Throw off the chains, call off the dogs, we're launched, we're outa here!

Mark Rudiger

Leg One
Headwinds and the Doldrums

Two minutes before the start of the Volvo Ocean Race, all eight boats were even on the line as they jockeyed for advantage. With 32,700 miles of racing ahead one would think a slight lead would not make a difference. But all 97 competitors from 16 countries were mindful that Paul Cayard on *EF Language* won the start in 1997 and went on to win leg one and the overall title. In fact, in six of seven Whitbreads, the team that won leg one went on to win the whole race.

The Volvo Ocean Race organizers did a good job opening a clear zone for the racing fleet, but immediately after the start all hell broke loose. The V.O.60s accelerated by setting their asymmetrical spinnakers in 15 knots of wind. Within 2 minutes an armada of over 400 craft ranging from dinghies to huge ferries sprinted into the best position to watch the race. It looked like the running of the bulls in Pamplona where the townspeople are all mixed in with the bulls. Everyone on the water suddenly became an ocean racer.

My view was as a guest aboard the German boat, *illbruck*. American skipper John Kostecki drove with a cool hand. He had a chance to win the start but chose to be conservative when Grant Dalton aboard *Amer Sports*

One slid to leeward. Assisting Dalton was American Dee Smith, noted for his hyper-aggressive style. Kostecki, understandably, did not want to risk a foul.

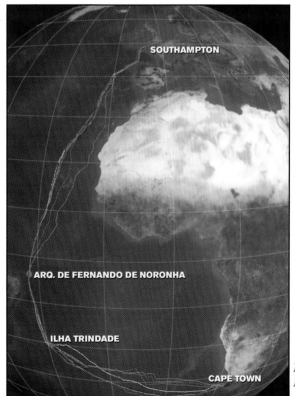

Leg one of the Volvo Ocean Race from Southampton to Cape Town. Distance 7,350 nautical miles.

Once off the line, *illbruck* passed three boats in minutes by accelerating on huge waves timed with the puffs. The wind quickly built to 24 knots. This newest generation of V.O.60s handled like Lasers. It is no accident that every team includes champion dinghy sailors on their roster. Kostecki's crew was impressive. Between them they had 12 previous Whitbread racers, and 10 America's Cup sailors, and all had grown up racing small boats.

Dalton emerged as the leader even though his reacher halyard jammed for 4 minutes during a spinnaker change. Both *Assa Abloy* and *Amer Sports Too* blew out spinnakers in the first 30 minutes.

illbruck appeared to have a speed edge in these conditions. *SEB* was good when the wind was lighter but slowed relative to the other boats as the wind increased. After 15 miles, *Tyco*, *News Corp*, *Amer Sports Too*, and *Assa Abloy* dropped back. To give their boat added stability (and speed), the water tanks aboard *illbruck* were filled and emptied on every puff, which seemed to be a lot of work.

In the interviews with the skippers before the start I was impressed by how respectful they were of each other, how thorough their preparations were, and how

djuice, Day 15

yeeehaa, 21 knots . . .

go, go, go, go . . .

Wouter Verbraak

View from the top of the mast of SEB *after picking up a new headboard car off Madeira.*

uncertain they were about how they would perform against the others. Grant Dalton, now on his seventh round-the-world race, was mentioned as a formidable opponent by every other skipper. Dalton has an easy-going style but is very methodical.

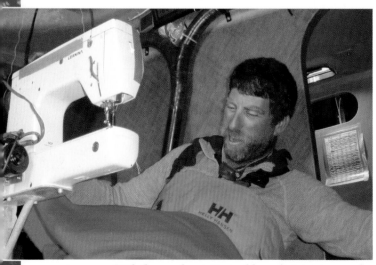

With the weather getting colder a djuice *crew member sews the blankets together to make sleeping bags.*

The catastrophic events of September 11 just 2 weeks before the start definitely had an effect on the weekend, with a somber mood around the docks. On the morning of race day, the Australian-sponsored entry, *News Corp*, flew an American flag from her forestay. A second banner underneath read "from sea to shining sea." *illbruck's* mainsail featured an inscription, "SAILING FOR FREEDOM." Just before leaving, over 10,000 fans crowding Ocean Village observed 1 minute of silence. *Assa Abloy* left the dock with crew members holding the flags of the eight countries represented by the crew.

After 20 miles, it was time for me to depart *illbruck.* A tender picked me up, and I waved as the fleet disappeared over the horizon. It was a beautiful start.

The first week was hell as the fleet pounded upwind in 25 knots. The V.O.60s were designed to sail downwind, so it was a cruel beginning, and many of the crew were seasick.

After their good start, *SEB* dropped back to sixth, then moved back up to first on day two. It was clear

Amer Sports One, Day Eight

Back in the hunt today after the wind Gods smiled on us this morning.

Grant Dalton

SEB, Day 13

We have been attacked by flying fish in a way not seen before. They arrive hundreds at a time and quite a few of them end up on the boat, even inside. Tony Mutter, our sail coordinator and watch captain, found one nearly dead fish under the sails inside the boat. He refused to remove it with the explanation that he hates flying fish. One thing is for sure though; he will find a fish in his sleeping bag if I know these guys right.

Gunnar Krantz

Amer Sports One crew out on the rail at the start of the Volvo Ocean Race.

right from the start that lead changes would take place frequently. Day four brought bad luck for *SEB* and *djuice*, when both broke their mainsail headboard cars, and dropped them to the back of the fleet. *Amer Sports Too* was also well behind at this point after blowing out several sails at the start. It was still a blustery 25 knots, briefly creating mean 9 to 18-foot seas, when *illbruck* surged into the lead. When the wind finally moderated, the lead shifted over and over.

Tyco, Day 17

The equator . . . duty to be paid to Neptune by three crew . . . apparently the dues are expected to be severe as the lord of the deep is not in good humor.

Damion Foxall

illbruck made the first bold tactical move of the race by sailing east on day 10. The gamble worked. Surprisingly, *SEB* sailed even further east and took the lead. It is always interesting when a boat takes a flyer, how good things look initially, but it rarely works out. *SEB* could not get back to the west to consolidate her lead, and dropped back to seventh. As the fleet sailed on toward the equator and a date with King Neptune, a parade developed, with *Amer Sports One* 60 miles behind the leader.

illbruck, Day 17

I saw Stu "waffler" Bettany busy getting the King Neptune crown ready, and a bucket on deck contains some brew. We are expecting the visit from the King of the Seas tomorrow morning.

Juan Vila

Dolphins have been a sign of safe passage for mariners for centuries.

Leg One Results

Position	Yacht	Elapsed Time	Leg Points	Overall Points	Overall Standings
1	illbruck	31 days 6 hours 19 minutes	8	8	1
2	Amer Sports One	31 days 8 hours 20 minutes	7	7	2
3	News Corp	32 days 15 hours 57 minutes	6	6	3
4	Tyco	33 days 16 hours 37 minutes	5	5	4
5	Assa Abloy	34 days 18 hours 11 minutes	4	4	5
6	SEB	36 days 19 hours 35 minutes	3	3	6
7	djuice	37 days 5 hours 0 minutes	2	2	7
8	Amer Sports Too	37 days 11 hours 20 minutes	1	1	8

It was a rough leg for *djuice*. A rendezvous was planned after their headboard car failure, so their shore crew chartered a 55-foot ketch and anchored a mile offshore, as the rules required. Naturally, it happened in the dark of night. Supplies included a headboard car for the mainsail, parts to repair the water maker, and a few gallons of diesel fuel. In less than 2 minutes it was done. A pit stop at sea, thanks to GPS, radio, e-mail, and good planning.

On day 23, *SEB* broke her headboard car again and dropped to last. On the same day *Amer Sports One* split with the fleet and headed south after rounding Fernando de Noronha. The move was brilliant, and Dalton took the lead. Dalton was his usual modest self. "South is king. It's really a rule of thumb. There is no weather map that really even says that, so we're just trying to apply some experience to what is a tricky part of the ocean and we have a fragile lead. We take it with due humbleness. We've been a bit lucky. But luck always tends to go around and we'll pay our dues at some point."

Over the next week the rich got richer as the fleet sailed into more wind. *Amer Sports One* kept the lead but their key spinnaker blew apart. As an aside, Dalton's wife delivered a baby girl. "I got a bit of a shock really," he said. "I'm just delighted."

As the days wore on, tight freeze-dried food rations wore down the crews, yet offered a limitless topic for conversation. The humorous approach to adversity came through via e-mail.

Meanwhile *illbruck* moved from 40 miles behind the leader to just 10 miles back, and Dalton was wishing he still had that key spinnaker. At the end of the long, 7,350-mile leg, *illbruck* passed *Amer Sports One* in 20 knots of breeze to take the lead, arriving in Cape

illbruck races for the finish to win leg one. She seems to power over the waves with her double head rig.

illbruck, Day 23

It seems the food crimes onboard continue. Yesterday there was some double dipping on the chocolate-covered granola bars. Of course the finger was pointed at Cheese [Dirk De Ridder] after he displayed his liking of Nuttella.

Mark Christensen

djuice, Day 27

Jacques [Vincent], the squirrel, has been saving noodles and energy bars from the moment we left Southampton and is protecting his secret hiding place, his crew bag, with his life.

Micke [Mikael Lundh] the trader is making deals non-stop with as many people as possible. A smart move from his side has been to save the two cans of cola we got at our stop at Fernando de Noronha. He has found a brilliant victim in Espen [Guttormsen], who is known to go to extremities in order to get the little pleasure from a small sip of cola. Christen [Horn Johannessen] is still very vulnerable with his chocolate addiction and found himself begging for a pack of noodles the other day because of too many trades for chocolate in happier times.

Finally there are those who trust their higher fat percentage to go all the way.

Wouter Verbraak

Amer Sports Too, *Day 34*

The more raw our lives get as we run out of supplies, the more you realise you can do without.

You can get by on less food, and you see you don't have to have wet wipes, and your spotty botty does not really need baby powder. It doesn't matter there is little to no toothpaste and the deodorant has all gone. As long as you have a little food in the belly, a dry bunk to crawl into, and a great team around you, you're gonna do just fine.

Bridget Suckling

Southern Right Whales off Cape Town at the end of leg one.

Tyco, *Day 33*

The wind gods have played a few tricks this leg so far but they have saved their best 'till last. The boat crashes into the trough behind the wave and leaves everything including the keel vibrating from the shock loads . . . the big 6-ton bulb moving around on the fin for several seconds afterwards during which time the talking stops and a few nervous glances are exchanged.

Steve Hayles

News Corp, *Day 29*

I am sure that every parent who has taken their children on a long trip will appreciate what every navigator is going through, right now, with the end-less questions: When will we be there? What time will we arrive? Where are we staying? I am hungry . . .

Ross Field

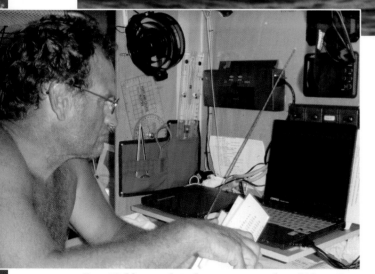

Ross Field at work in the nav station aboard News Corp *plotting the best place to cross the Doldrums and the optimum angle in and out.*

SEB, Day 34

My calculation says that when we have finished this leg, we will have sailed all the upwind work there is to do in this race. Normally, there should be between 10 and 12 percent of close-hauled sailing in the Volvo Ocean Race, approximately 3000 to 4000 miles. It is good to have that over and done with, I can now look forward to the other legs with no beats at all.

Gunnar Krantz

V.O.60 yachts sit ashore in their cradles awaiting maintenance during the Cape Town stopover. The boats look like thoroughbreds ready to take off from the gate.

Town after 31 days, 6 hours, beating *Amer Sports One* by a mere 2 hours. Two protests threatened to mar *illbruck's* win. One by *Assa Abloy* for improper use of a weather web site, was withdrawn; another by the Race Committee, for using a weed cutter, resulted in a small fine but no loss of points.

The crews of both *illbruck* and *Amer Sports One* were overjoyed with their performances. "Preparation helped but we have the right people, and that is the secret of our success," said a delighted John Kostecki. ⚑▶

Amer Sports One, Day 27

Now that we have had a sniff of our nose in front, the competitive instincts take over and you get mad as hell.

Grant Dalton

John Kostecki and his illbruck *crew celebrate their victory at the end of leg one. Two years of hard work payed off for* illbruck.

SEB, Day 10

We look forward to the next firehose session tomorrow
and the following days. This, again, means face mask on,
head down and just go.

Magnus Woxen,
on setting a new 24-hour record of 459 nautical miles

Leg Two
Cape Town to Sydney

The sails stacked to windward provide relief to the SEB crew from the spray, but the water to leeward still gets everyone wet. When the boat is sailing at 30 knots the spray hurts—goggles protect the eyes.

illbruck, Day 16

Two words to keep in mind when racing through the Southern Ocean: respect and patience. Remember and abide by these concepts and you will continue to have safe and pleasant passages through the harshest waters known to mankind.

Stu Bannatyne

Leg Two
Southern Ocean Surfing

Technically not an ocean, the fierce body of water known to sailors as the Southern Ocean is actually the confluence of the Atlantic, Pacific, and Indian Oceans. The wind and waves are ferocious, but in spite of the conditions, sailors thrive here because the boats sail fast. Indeed, for many skippers, sailing well through the Southern Ocean is a major accomplishment in itself. With speed, however, comes danger. Everyone was mindful of the horrors of past round-the-world races that included broken masts and rudders, frostbite, near sinkings, snapped keels, injuries, fatigue, and even death.

An impressive flotilla was on hand to watch the Volvo Ocean Race fleet depart Cape Town. Table Mountain looked like a watchful guardian as the fleet headed south under the lee of one of the world's most famous landfalls. On the first night the sailors were hammered by 35-knot winds and steep waves, a cruel way to start the 6,550-mile leg to Sydney, Australia.

Aboard *illbruck*, skipper John Kostecki could feel something was wrong with his boat, with *SEB* nearby and pulling away. *illbruck* felt sluggish and her highly trained crew searched for the problem, discovering that the bow compartment was rapidly filling with water. Kostecki was cool under pressure: with the help of the shore crew the leak was located near the foredeck hatch. Sails were lowered, the damage repaired, the boat bailed out, and then the crew rehoisted the sails and took off.

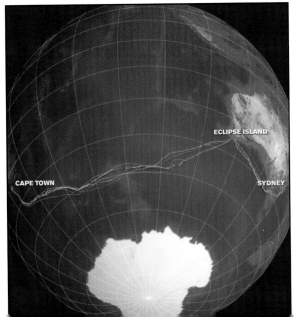

SEB navigator Marcel van Triest couldn't believe the awful sight of *illbruck* wallowing in the waves, "They are about three boatlengths behind us. Sails luffing in the wind. Bow down. Doesn't look very good."

The *illbruck* team had prepared for over 2 years and this incident was a test of the crew's resourcefulness. Over the radio Kostecki described the setback with his usual low-key candor: "The front compartment was filled with very cold water and at that point we were taking on water a lot faster than we could get rid of it. Because it was so rough the bow would go under on every wave so that more water would be coming in."

By the time *illbruck* resumed racing, the rest of the fleet was 20 miles ahead. Sked after sked the crew gained on the leaders. The progress gave the crew encouragement, and *illbruck* would carry this momentum for the next 3 weeks.

On day four *Tyco* lost her steerage; the rudder was falling apart. The seas were still big, making a repair a difficult task. With *Tyco* in the front row at the time, it was a disappointing blow to skipper Kevin Shoebridge:

Leg two from Cape Town to Sydney. Distance 6,550 nautical miles.

Amer Sports Too, Day Five

There it was, standing still and tranquil, a statement of strength, a huge white glistening iceberg right in front of us, bang on our course.

Emma Westmacott

The crew wearing heavy weather gear and face masks aboard Amer Sports Too. *The veteran round-the-world sailors reported seeing extraordinary amounts of ice, especially during their second trip to the Southern Ocean after Auckland.*

"Our rudder shaft between the two bearings sheared off some of the carver on the front of the rudder stock. Then last night we heard a really loud bang and now the rudder is in danger of snapping off inside the boat directly above the lower bearing. There is no way we can use the rudder. We've dropped all our sails and it is highly unlikely that we'll be doing any more racing on this leg that's for sure. It's more of a situation now of not risking the boat or risking people."

Tyco made her way to Port Elizabeth on South Africa's south coast and the boat was shipped to Sydney for leg three.

The rest of the fleet arrived in the Southern Ocean on day five. It was cold, wet, and fast. *News Corp* headed south and sailed 447 miles in a 24-hour period. On day seven *News Corp* broke the 24-hour record with a 450.13-mile run. The conditions were wild, and below deck was a nightmare. Crews reported wet sleeping bags and extreme discomfort. The reports from the boats were philosophical:

"It's been a trip full of forest fires so far. We run around with a shovel throwing dirt on each little flare up and then move onto the next. The only trouble is, some we didn't put out properly and then they flare up into bigger problems. Perhaps fire is not the right analogy because if there was any more water around we would have sunk."—Mark Christensen, *illbruck*

Tyco *ploughs through the waves at the start of leg two from Cape Town to Sydney. The man standing on the gooseneck seems unfazed as he checks the bend of the mast. Is the rest of the crew enjoying life?*

Tyco, News Corp, illbruck, djuice, *and* Amer Sports One *carving through the fog an hour after the start of leg two.*

The Beach Boys were correct, "Catch a wave and you're sitting on top of the world." The crew seemed to take the speed in stride.

Kilpatrick, was suffering from a painful intestinal blockage. The Australian Air Force dropped antibiotics and morphine from an RAAF Orion. For 8 days Kilpatrick was only able to ingest liquids, and he was lucky that navigator Roger Nilson was also a medical doctor.

Meanwhile, *SEB* broke the 24-hour record again with an astounding 460-mile run. It would be a high point of the *SEB* campaign.

Then the wind dropped and the lead pack compressed, with *Assa Abloy*, *SEB*, and the rapidly gaining *illbruck*, jibing frequently. Two days later a high-pressure system swallowed the fleet, and five boats dueled close together. *Amer Sports One*, languishing 134 miles behind, closed to just 26 miles in 3 days.

Unlike most ocean racers that have little speed differences, the V.O.60s can make up a huge distance in a short time. At this point the distance between the top five boats amounted to only 14 miles!

illbruck was the first to round Eclipse Island off the southwest coast of Australia, an amazing recovery after her earlier problems. Later that day Kilpatrick was taken off *Amer Sports One* by a small boat and delivered to a hospital in Albany, Australia. He soon recovered but did not sail again in the Volvo Ocean Race. At the same time, Marcel van Triest received the

"Sea water temperature is now 6 degrees and the Southern Ocean gray is spreading all over the place. Everything looks, and is, gray down here. Being here for the fourth time it is all easy to recognize. Can't say I have anything but a hate/love relationship with this place, in that order."—Gunnar Krantz, *SEB*

Amer Sports Too, Day 10

We dress like roly-poly Michelin men and cannot immediately identify each other under all the gear without hearing a voice, recognizing the color of the eyes, or checking the name written on the jacket.

Genevieve White

bunch of guys."—Ross Field, *News Corp*

On day 10 *Amer Sports One* called Race Headquarters and asked for assistance. Amid the terrible conditions an American crew member, Keith

"Remember, with all the discomfort, we love this place—strong winds, wild rides, being a little on edge for days and sailing with a good

illbruck celebrates her second victory after winning leg two from Cape Town to Sydney.

Leg Two Results

Position	Yacht	Elapsed Time	Leg Points	Overall Points	Overall Standings
1	illbruck	22 days 13 hours 22 minutes	8	16	1
2	SEB	22 days 14 hours 35 minutes	7	10	4
3	News Corp	22 days 15 hours 17 minutes	6	12	2
4	djuice	22 days 19 hours 43 minutes	5	7	5
5	Amer Sports One	22 days 19 hours 50 minutes	4	11	3
6	Assa Abloy	22 days 22 hours 31 minutes	3	7	6
7	Amer Sports Too	26 days 4 hours 59 minutes	2	3	8
8	Tyco	Retired from leg	1	6	7

unfortunate news that his mother had died. At Eclipse Island he literally dove off the side of *SEB* and traveled back to Holland for the funeral.

As *illbruck* passed Eclipse Island, she picked up some much-needed parts, allowing *SEB* to regain the lead. With Eclipse behind them, *SEB* and *illbruck* headed south, while *Assa Abloy* and *News Corp* tracked 60 miles north.

When the wind filled in from astern at 35 knots, the southern-positioned boats felt new wind first and took off. *SEB* led but suffered a severe broach, costing them their masthead spinnaker and the lead.

In the notorious Bass Strait, the fleet was greeted by another big blow. Broaches were common; *djuice*, *News Corp*, and *Amer Sports One* all had wipeouts and both Grant Dalton and Ross Field suffered cracked ribs.

A spectacular wipeout by *Amer Sports One* was captured by the film team of George Johns, Steve Ancsell, and Rick Tomlinson. Under spinnaker, in 40-plus knots, the short-handed *Amer Sports One* crew careened out of control. The highly experienced Dalton, strapped below in his bunk, knew his boat was in trouble and braced himself. The hull spun into a wild slow-motion jibe as the helmsman desperately tried to get the boat back on course. But the rudder was out of the water. *Amer Sports One* lay on her side for minutes as the crew struggled to drop the spinnaker and right the boat, while skipping over the

waves at 3 knots. The riveting pictures would surely grace sporting clip reels for years to come. Dalton was taken off in a stretcher.

illbruck entered Sydney Harbor triumphantly to win her second leg, and amazingly, the top six boats finished within 12 hours of each other. *illbruck's* afterguard was ecstatic to be in Sydney as they reflected on the tough leg they had just completed. "It was definitely the toughest leg in the Volvo or former Whitbread Race that I've ever done. It's a brutal race.

Assa Abloy, Day Three

I left my girl friend, good food, a dry bed and a hot shower to bang around out here struggling with wet Kevlar sails and twelve smelly guys.

Stu Wilson

illbruck, Day 10

Reaching, wet, cold, bail, eat, and sleep. Life is so simple.

Mark Christensen

It takes a toll on your body," said John Kostecki. Richard Clarke added, "Complete and utter hell. It was a battle from start to finish. I've never been so tired, so fatigued, so cold in my life."

After recovering from their wipeout, *Amer Sports One* finished fifth, with *Amer Sports Too* coming in 3 days behind them.

Amer Sports One broaches out of control off the coast of Sydney. Skipper Grant Dalton was already injured and due to be taken off by stretcher when they docked in Sydney. The boat was moving sideways at 3 knots.

SEB, Day 10

In the absolute inferno of wind and waves that followed I could only hear the boys under the cascades of water. Shouting, pushing, and just going wild. Top speed? 34.79 on the dial.

Gunnar Krantz

The Southern Ocean is not what it used to be. It's too easy, too little wind. Too much sunshine and too warm. Something is wrong.

Knut Frostad, djuice

As they make their way from Cape Town to Sydney in the heavy pounding seas, the crew of SEB try to keep dry and warm as freezing spray engulfs them on deck. It's just as wet down below.

Leg Three
Sydney to Auckland

Tyco, Day Four

We can start getting ready for a New Year's Eve bash onboard. Maybe a protein bar and a strong cup of coffee.

Kevin Shoebridge

News Corp, Day Five

Beautiful night, full moon, cool on deck, quiet and smooth seas. There's the odd click of a winch, a flap of a sail, and a loud snore from Barney Walker, but that's the only noise. It's a vast contrast from the bash and crash we have had over the past few days.

Ross Field

Leg Three
Pit Stop in Hobart

Prior to the start, in what appeared to be a practical joke played by some good-natured ocean racers, the Volvo Ocean Race fleet sailed out of Sydney in no wind but with their storm sails set. With vivid memories of the 1998 Sydney to Hobart Race storm and the hard blow on the way to Hobart in 2000, the sailors knew it was no joke. The exercise was a requirement of the Cruising Club of Australia Race Committee's commitment to safety.

At the pre-race meeting, the crews seemed to pay unusually close attention to the safety briefing. Little did they know that 8 hours later they would be facing a fearsome waterspout.

Adding to the gravity of the start, each skipper dropped a wreath in the water in memory of the late Sir Peter Blake soon after leaving the dock on December 26, 2001. Pirates in South America had murdered Blake, a legend to all 97 sailors, just weeks before the start.

The course for leg three was unusual for ocean racing. The Volvo Ocean Race fleet was scheduled to join the 630-mile Sydney to Hobart Race fleet, but with a twist: the boats would restart in Hobart after a 3-hour

pit stop. The idea was unpopular with the skippers. Grant Dalton's resignation to the concept surfaced: "The rules say we have to go to Hobart so we will do it."

The scene at Sydney Harbor added to the surreal atmosphere, with heavy smoke covering the city and

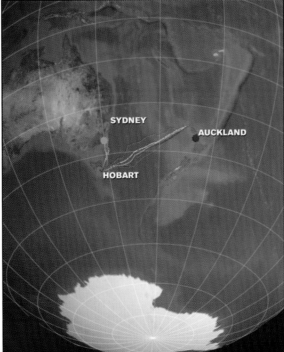

coast from a series of brush fires raging out of control. The smoke stretched all the way across the Tasman Sea to New Zealand. Breathing was uncomfortable and the sky gave off an ominous glow.

The V.O.60s started about 300 meters ahead of the rest of the fleet. The wind died a few minutes after the gun in one of the slowest Sydney to Hobart starts in memory. *Assa Abloy* was hurt most; the boat looked like a Monet painting with its drooping sail. It was a tough initiation for American boatspeed specialist and world champion Chris Larson, who was recruited to help *Assa Abloy* after humble fifth- and sixth-place finishes in the first two legs.

News Corp won a quick $10,000 by sailing out the Sydney Heads first. Soon the wind filled, and *illbruck* set six different sail combinations in an hour, the crew reacting instantly to subtle shifts.

Eight hours after the start, a waterspout formed directly in the path of the fleet. Many of the crews prudently lowered their sails. The riveting photographs shot by the sailors were broadcast around the world by CNN. One skipper issued lifejackets as the tornado approached. *News Corp* veteran Gordon Macguire

Leg three from Sydney to Auckland. Distance 2,050 nautical miles.

Amer Sports Too, Day Seven

A lightning storm burnt into our memory for the beginning of 2002. It was our version of fireworks only a bit more dangerous and we were stuck in the middle with nowhere to go.

Lisa McDonald

The crew of illbruck *wisely wears safety harnesses as they slog upwind.*

admitted, "I was generally frightened." The experience of the Southern Ocean on leg two no doubt helped everyone deal with the tornado safely.

A "southerly change," as it is known in Australia, greeted the fleet with gusto. For the next 36 hours 35 to 40-knot headwinds and vicious waves made life unbearable. The decision to race to Hobart was questioned by everyone, and the whole fleet had problems. *Amer Sports One* could not operate her water ballast system and dropped back. *djuice* filled with water in much the same way that *illbruck* did on leg two, and lost her electronics in the flood. *Amer Sports Too* broke her forestay and had to jury rig, and *SEB's* rudder

Amer Sports One, Day Six

You probably wonder what happens onboard on New Years Eve? Not much except that I just noticed the whole on-going watch wearing big, black, plastic sunglasses with a huge pink nose attached to them. I find it hard to believe someone is going to open a bottle of champagne at midnight . . . but you never know, perhaps a bottle is stacked away in someone's minimal crew bag.

Roger Nilson

A waterspout—tornado—came through illbruck, Assa Abloy and ourselves giving us wind up to 58 knots . . . long vertical round spinning cloud charged towards us with the bottom of it sucking up water. There was nowhere to go. —Ross Field, News Corp

We had a chance to come close to a huge waterspout. It looked like a gigantic vacuum cleaner coming down to suck away all the tiny boats littering the water. It was formed very quickly and picked up speed immediately. —Gunnar Krantz, SEB

It was an impressive sight, literally turning the surface of the water into foam, but an unnerving one as we monitored its erratic progress. —Steve Hayles, Tyco

We encountered an experience that we will remember for the rest of our lives. The wind built to 50 knots as the waterspout got closer to us. It appeared to be passing to windward of us, but then suddenly it changed course again. Now it was only 400 meters away, blowing 60 knots and this huge spiraling cloud was nearly on top of us. We had a helpless feeling, where this freak of nature was chasing us down. —John Kostecki, illbruck

Several boats took their sails down as the waterspout passed within a mile. Crews reported that the noise was deafening

SEB had to retire from leg three due to rudder problems. Rodney Ardern inspects SEB's broken rudder below deck after it was taken off and hauled into the boat.

ripped out of the boat, leaving a gaping hole. While it is unclear why the rudder broke away, it was most likely the result of hitting a submerged object or a whale. Whatever the cause, the damage forced Gunnar Krantz to retire from the leg. *SEB* returned to Australia for repairs.

Bass Strait off Australia's southeast coast has the reputation of being a nasty stretch of water and it lived up to its reputation. It was so rough it was difficult to eat, and the crews were thrown around like dice in a shaker. Many were seasick.

As the fleet finally neared Hobart the wind went light, causing positions to reshuffle frequently. The changes in fortune were dramatic: *Amer Sports One* jumped to second from seventh, and *illbruck* fell to fourth after leading for 2 days. *Assa Abloy* was in sixth with twenty-four miles left, but sailed up the Derwent River first. Skipper Neal McDonald, navigator Mark

Assa Abloy, Day Six

After reading the latest article on the Volvo Ocean Race web site, I realize it is out in the open now . . . Hi, my name is Rudi, and uh, I'm a chronic gambler. I guess I have been in denial for some time but now it is obvious, after our move out of Hobart and previous legs that I must confront the issue head on.

Mark Rudiger

*Assa Abloy **reaching in the setting sun of New Year's Day 2002. Skipper Neal McDonald (right) looks very content** with Assa Abloy **in the lead.***

Leg Three Results

Position	Yacht	Elapsed Time	Leg Points	Overall Points	Overall Standings
1	Assa Abloy	8 days 11 hours 50 minutes	8	15	4
2	Amer Sports One	8 days 13 hours 39 minutes	7	18	2
3	Tyco	8 days 14 hours 48 minutes	6	12	5
4	illbruck	8 days 14 hours 52 minutes	5	21	1
5	News Corp	8 days 14 hours 54 minutes	4	16	3
6	djuice	8 days 17 hours 46 minutes	3	10	7
7	Amer Sports Too	10 days 5 hours 57 minutes	2	5	8
8	SEB	Retired from leg	1	11	6

Rudiger, and Volvo Ocean Race rookie Chris Larson later admitted they might have been "a little lucky."

The crews were used to going ashore for a good meal and taking plenty of time to catch up on sleep when they came into port, but this pit stop was different. It was critical that the racers remained focussed, as they only had 3 hours before they set off again. The restart in Hobart for each boat was given in the order and with the time difference of the finish.

Tyco *steams into Auckland to take third place.*

Assa Abloy and *Amer Sports One* made a bold move to the north. Unfortunately, *Amer Sports Too* had to return to the dock after their restart for repairs to the rudder. The boat was hauled for the fix and the crew lost another 19 hours.

The northern strategy proved to be a winner. *Assa Abloy* stretched to a 37-mile lead over *Amer Sports One*, who had a 109-mile lead over *News Corp* in third. *Tyco* and *illbruck* were close behind. Knut Frostad's frustration grew aboard *djuice*—he had sailed south looking for wind and was now well behind in sixth place.

Scary thunderstorms pestered *Assa Abloy* on New Year's Eve, but she was speeding ahead at a brisk 14 knots, until the next day when the leaders sailed into powerful headwinds, with constant sail changes exhausting the crews. On top of that three men were out of commission with ailments ranging from a badly bruised back and kidney stones to a possible urinary infection.

There is a saying in New Zealand that if you don't like the weather, wait 5 minutes and it will change. In fact, you can experience all four seasons in 1 hour. As *Assa Abloy* and *Amer Sports One* approached Cape Reinga on the northwest coast of New Zealand the wind disappeared. To make matters worse, a 3-knot current on the nose made progress excruciatingly slow.

The two boats were able to sneak around Cape Reinga and North Cape for the 200-mile sprint to Auckland. For a New Zealander, arriving first into Auckland is one of sailing's biggest thrills, but Grant Dalton ended up second on his home waters.

As dawn gave way to a gray day, Television New Zealand broadcast pictures of an intense three-way battle for third on a giant screen in Viaduct Basin. Fans eagerly awaited the arrival of their favorite boats, as New Zealand sailors populated each one.

illbruck, *Tyco*, and *News Corp* had been locked in a three-way battle for 5 days. Two-time America's Cup winning navigator Peter Isler aboard *News Corp* used every trick in his thick book but could not find a way to pass.

Kevin Shoebridge erased the demons of leg two with a well-earned third; *illbruck* was fourth and *News Corp* fifth. A dejected crew on *djuice* arrived 3 hours later. According to Stig Westergaard, "This is not a good result and we didn't sail well. I think we basically knew where we made the mistakes and we can only learn from it and go forward from there. But it is not satisfying." The women aboard *Amer Sports Too* came in 36 hours later to a big, admiring, and festive crowd.

The sailors would have 23 days to prepare for their return to the Southern Ocean and rounding of Cape Horn—the windiest headland in the world. 🏴

January 4, 2002. Assa Abloy's crew celebrates its victory in leg three. In a tribute to Sir Peter Blake they wore "lucky red socks."

Amer Sports Too, Day 8

After a 4-hour watch you come down below with red, watery, stinging, salt sore eyes: a nose so cold and dribbly you think it may fall off or at least you hope it might.

Lisa McDonald

Leg Four
Auckland to Rio de Janeiro

The crew of Amer Sports Too *trim the sails in heavy weather.*

SEB

Passing growlers (chunks of floating ice) at 25 knots at night within a couple feet makes me nervous.
Three times we have passed growlers the size of cars so close that the white water around it touches the
hull. Russian roulette is probably safer than this. We had 21 large icebergs on radar one night.

Gunnar Krantz

Leg Four
Ice in the Southern Ocean

Auckland, New Zealand—proudly known as the "City of Sails"—proved to be a terrific stopover. Every boat had substantial maintenance performed in anticipation of their second leg of racing in the Southern Ocean. On January 27, 2002, a large spectator fleet was on hand to wish the fleet a safe voyage. For the first 2 days the wind was light, the waters flat, and the boats close—a literal calm before the storm.

Among the new crew was Paul Cayard, who joined *Amer Sports One* as a strategist and helmsman. Before the leg Cayard said: "I'm definitely a guest on board, here just for this leg. Grant's got everything the way he wants it so it's not really my show. The job I'm doing on the boat, though, is quite similar to what I've done in previous races. I'll be working with Roger Nilson with the weather and the routing and that is exactly what I did on *EF*."

In 1998, when Cayard was on his way to victory in the Whitbread, fellow St. Francis Yacht Club sailor John Kostecki was back in the fleet aboard *Chessie Racing*. The duo later teamed up for the America's Cup trials in Auckland for the 2000 match. Right from the outset of leg four *Amer Sports One* (with Cayard on board) and *illbruck* (commanded by

Kostecki) began a 5,000-mile duel. There is no doubt that the personal competition between two of America's best sailors raised the bar for both boats.

Predicting the weather on this leg was important for success. The tactical quandary was how far south to go. In the Southern Ocean the winds are stronger the closer you get to Antarctica, but it can also be more dangerous depending on the amount of ice. Every team was secretive about its strategic plans.

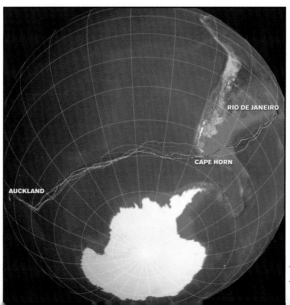

Leg four from Auckland to Rio de Janeiro.
Distance 6,700 nautical miles.

There was some shuffling on the third day as the first cold front swept across the fleet. On day five a stronger cold front arrived, and *Amer Sports One* was the first to jibe onto port heading southeast. The rest of the group continued on their southerly course. One day later, *Amer Sports One* was disappointed that the early jibe did not produce a big gain. Cayard wrote via e-mail of the difficulty in making decisions. "The amount of information now available is unbelievable. You can definitely keep two people busy 24 hours a day analyzing this stuff. Luckily Roger, who is 50 plus, only sleeps 4 hours a day but I, at a youthful 42, still need my 6 hours per day or I get grumpy. So we just have to make do with 38 man hours per day on this stuff."

On day seven *illbruck* emerged in the lead. Skipper John Kostecki and navigator Juan Vila positioned *illbruck* perfectly for a new weather pattern. The *illbruck* crew was relentless, flying a spinnaker in 40 knots of wind. It was cold, wet, and nasty, and the crews slept in their foul weather gear. For the first time in the race they started seeing lots of ice.

As the fleet pressed on the temperature dropped. It was miserable. Veterans like Grant Dalton, Ross Field, and Marcel van Triest sent messages back that there was more ice than they had ever seen in this desolate part of the world.

Luckily, at this time of the year there is considerable daylight, so the large icebergs slowly bouncing in the swells were easy to see by eye and on radar. The real danger was the threat of running into a growler or bergy bit. These relatively small chunks of ice sit just on the surface of the water, and are most prevalent to leeward of a larger iceberg. The V.O.60s were sailing at speeds well above 20 knots so a collision would have been catastrophic. John Kostecki knew how to handle things: "We've got an iceberg on the target here, looks like its getting pretty close, 3 miles bearing 85. So looks like we are going to go underneath this one. Hopefully there won't be any growlers. We've got to keep our eyes open."

Scientists reported that unusually warm temperatures were releasing staggering amounts of ice from the Antarctic Peninsula, including a section of ice shelf the size of Rhode Island that dissolved into the ocean. E-mails from the boats revealed high anxiety. Fear was a constant companion, but no crew throttled back.

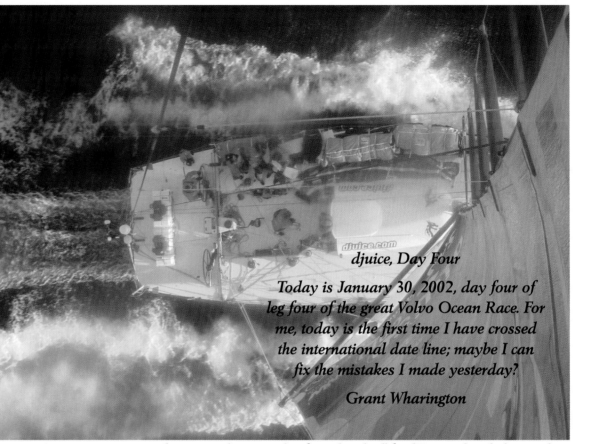

djuice, Day Four

Today is January 30, 2002, day four of leg four of the great Volvo Ocean Race. For me, today is the first time I have crossed the international date line; maybe I can fix the mistakes I made yesterday?

Grant Wharington

At this moment djuice *is sailing faster than the ill-fated* Titanic *when she hit an iceberg.*

Crew were constantly sent aloft during sail changes. This view is from Amer Sports One.

Charting a course through the ice was a gamble, particularly at night. Helmsmen often had to make sharp changes of course to avoid the ice.

News Corp reported a collision at 21 knots. Ross Field was at the helm at the time: "I am worried. This is dangerous. There are icebergs everywhere." After the collision with the unknown object, *News Corp* headed north. The hull, keel, and rudder were all intact, but nine days later the rudder snapped off. They were not sure if the collision was to blame, but it was a long sail to Rio using the emergency rudder hanging off the stern and stubby tiller controlling it.

Amer Sports One came upon two huge bergs that they could not go around. The wind was too strong to

take the sail down or to jibe. It would be impossible to beat to windward and dangerous to sail to leeward because of the bergy bits. So they decided to sail between them—it must have been a frightening moment.

On day 12 *SEB* broached, and the boat rounded violently into the wind. *SEB* was designed with two hatches just behind the mast. The standard practice was to keep the windward hatch open for ventilation and the leeward hatch closed. During this broach, the boat spun around to windward. The open hatch, now on the leeward side, allowed a massive amount of seawater to rush below. The boat stayed on its side for what seemed like minutes. Finally the mast broke about 8 feet above

No sooner had we gotten the shredded spinnaker down than Roger Nilson yells up, two icebergs ahead, 4 miles. The width of the two bergs forced us to sail between them. This is not recommended in any book. We had a few tense moments there but we got through unscathed.

Paul Cayard

Gordon Maguire, helmsman of News Corp

I was on evening watch, and it's getting dark. Last light, everything's getting really dusty, it's foggy and you've got about 400 yards visibility. It's blowing 35 knots, you're doing 25 knots of boat speed, you're just hanging on the wheel, you haven't wiped out, everything is under control, it's just another day at the office. The navigator sticks his head up the hatch and says "Iceberg on the bow." You go "How far?" He says, "One mile." One mile at 25 knots, you don't even want to think about it. It's like 3 minutes and you're on top of it. When you're driving in those conditions you have what we call a 10-degree envelope to steer in. You can either go up 5 degrees or down 5 degrees and either side of that is a wipeout. The navigator comes back up, "Second iceberg, on the port bow." You're kidding? Is it the same iceberg? You're actually within a minute of arriving in this scenario and you're actualy not sure that these blips on the radar are one iceberg or two icebergs.

It happens to be two icebergs, but in the middle is a whole pile of melted ice. From the size of something you would drop in your drink, literally, to the size of a bus. The sea is covered in ice. You have a guy standing on your shoulder and he calls you, "Up," "Down" and you basically drive through this pack ice, picking out the big bits to miss as the small bits just bounce along the side of the boat and out the back. And all the time, you're doing 25 knots, the hammer is down fully, you are just rocking down. You are thinking, "If we hit something bigger than 6 or 8 feet across, then we will compromise the hull and go down." And then you pop out the other end of it and there is no more ice—there is no more anything. The other watch is coming up and you go down below and you take your gloves off and your feet are frozen and your hands are frozen, and you just curl up in your bunk and you just pretend you're not there.

Icebergs are easier to see in big waves because they bounce up and down.

the deck. For the second leg in a row *SEB* was forced to withdraw.

Gunnar Krantz was crushed: "We are quite devastated by the situation. We have had our share of bad luck already. Don't need to top it off with this dismasting. But it has happened. It is reality. We just have to deal with it." *SEB* made her way to South America under jury rig. Even with the small amount of sail area, she sailed at an impressive 8 knots.

Amer Sports Too got off to a slow start and dropped back steadily. After 2 weeks they were 550 miles behind the leader. Even with an extra crew member the women couldn't match the men's brute strength required to race these boats efficiently in such extreme conditions. Steering was exhausting, with helmsmen barely lasting 60 minutes at the wheel. Hands went numb, shoulders cramped.

In the face of 40 and 50-knot gusts under spinnaker, knockdowns were unavoidable. The narrow keels stalled easily, causing instability. And even the best helmsman was not fast enough—or strong enough—to anticipate the boat's moves.

illbruck was the first to round Cape Horn, and the sailors actually got to see this famous headland. Gale

Assa Abloy, Day 17

Yesterday morning as the sun rose from the eastern horizon, it silhouetted one of the nautical world's most famous landmarks, Cape Horn.

Mike Joubert

Race leader illbruck *rounds Cape Horn February 10, 2002.*

Crippled with a broken mast, SEB *approaches the Chilean coast under jury rig. Even with dramatically reduced sail* SEB *was moving at 8 knots.*

force winds buffet Cape Horn at least 1 week every month, and it is one of the windiest places on earth. As the storm fronts whip around South America, they smash into the Andes mountains. The air is too thin at the top of the mountains to hold moisture so the storm fronts find their escape route around the bottom of South America, at Cape Horn. More than 1,000 boats lie wrecked on the ocean bottom in the waters around Cape Horn.

The Volvo Ocean Race fleet was lucky. The wind was under 20 knots and the sky was clear, rewarding everyone with a nice view of Cape Horn. It is always

a relief to get past this landfall because the weather generally turns better as one heads north.

Onboard *djuice*, Stig Westergaard produced a small bottle of cognac to celebrate their successful rounding of the Horn, while crewmate Anthony Nossiter stripped down to streak laps around the boat. Others smoked cigars and waved farewell to the Southern Ocean. Not long after rounding the Horn the fleet sailed through Isla de los Estrados and encountered a powerful adverse current. *illbruck* broke through first and made a 20-mile gain. The next tactical question was which way to pass the Falkland Islands. *djuice* and *Amer Sports One* decided

Leg Four Results

Position	Yacht	Elapsed Time	Leg Points	Overall Points	Overall Standings
1	illbruck	23 days 5 hours 58 minutes	8	29	1
2	djuice	23 days 11 hours 52 minutes	7	17	6
3	Tyco	23 days 13 hours 4 minutes	6	18	5
4	Assa Abloy	23 days 14 hours 22 minutes	5	20	3
5	Amer Sports One	23 days 14 hours 50 minutes	4	22	2
6	News Corp	24 days 21 hours 55 minutes	3	19	4
7	Amer Sports Too	25 days 11 hours 6 minutes	2	7	8
8	SEB	Retired from leg	1	12	7

SEB, Day 14

The next squall hit us like a freight train. All the guys in the bunk were woken with a ton or so of 3-degree water flooding the cabin. The deck light illuminated the carnage. A sorry looking stump, a broken boom, most of the windward stack in the water and the bottom end of the mast hanging over the side.

Scott Beavis

to split with the fleet and sailed on the east side of the Falklands, and *djuice* gained 23 miles.

On day 17 *Amer Sports Too* passed the Horn in a near hurricane. After the rounding, the women stopped losing ground—clearly this boat was more

Tyco *under Sugarloaf Mountain finished third into Rio de Janeiro.*

competitive in moderate and light winds. As *Assa Abloy* passed through Isla de los Estrados, the wind was 38 knots and the current was 6 knots. The crew felt like they were whitewater rafting, not sailing. Skipper Neal McDonald showed a lot of leadership by going over the side himself to free the rudder of kelp.

On the way north the conditions became unstable. *Amer Sports One* fell into a hole and never recovered, a bitter disappointment for Grant Dalton and Paul Cayard. They had been in second place for 17 straight days.

After the big gain on the east side of the Falkland Islands, *djuice* headed west and continued to make substantial gains. The winds went light near Rio, and *illbruck* lost 25 miles as the fleet closed in, with four boats within 15 miles battling for second. It was difficult with numb hands, frostbitten feet, and the chill still lingering to concentrate in light, warm winds. *illbruck* finally coasted across the line for her third win, and an ecstatic Knut Frostad erased the demons of the first three legs by finishing second. Frostad was clever and took risks, but they worked. Immediately after finishing he said, "Unbelievable. Twelve hours ago there was 3 miles between second and fifth place. We made a pretty gutsy call in jibing a little later than the other guys and wanted to stay close to shore. I didn't sleep at all, I think, the last 30 hours."

Tyco finished with another third. This team was gaining momentum and confidence after its disappointment

on leg two. *Amer Sports One*, after sailing skillfully for most of the leg, arrived in Rio fifth. Paul Cayard tried to be upbeat: "It is very disappointing but we sailed really well and I think we raised the level of the game."

Roger Vaughan, writing for ESPN, summed up leg four nicely: "The ultimate in wild sleigh rides, the firehosing reaches through tunnels of bow waves that are unique to the Southern Ocean, have always been the lure of this race—the reason sailors return. But when seasoned veterans are horrified by speeding through minefields of ice, it might be time to reset the southern boundaries of the course."

illbruck *celebrates in typical Samba style on the podium in Rio after winning leg four.*

Leg Five

Rio de Janeiro to Miami

Amer Sports One *passed close to the rocks after the start of leg five, Rio de Janeiro to Miami.*

Tyco, Day Four

Reaching along in 15 knots of wind, with flat water and clear sunny skies: what more could we ask for?
(Apart from air conditioning, a bunk longer than 5 feet 5 inches, a decent book, and a 100-mile lead, that is.)

Steve Hayles

Leg Five
Heat at the Equator

The summer respite in Rio de Janeiro, Brazil, was surprisingly popular with the crews. The tropical heat thawed out the sailors after the brutal cold of the Southern Ocean and helped them mentally prepare for an equally daunting challenge, navigating through the maze of equatorial Doldrums. In previous races, capricious pockets of wind blew some boats to the front while others were inexplicably trapped in windless holes.

Even with the race more than half over, most skippers believed they still had a chance to place in the top three overall. Indeed, *illbruck's* speed advantage was suspect in light wind; roster changes on several boats were expected to help performance; and the unlucky boats—*SEB*, *Amer Sports Too*, *News Corp*, *Tyco*, and *djuice*—hoped their problems were over. The Doldrums can be the great equalizer.

At the start, several thousand spectator boats watched the V.O.60s sail to windward. It was hot, but mercifully, the 10 to 12-knot headwinds cooled everyone down. *djuice* was first through the turning gate;

their second-place finish in leg four obviously boosted the team's morale.

The boats had to choose whether they should risk heading further offshore to take advantage of more wind, or stay closer to land and simply sail fewer miles. The fleet swung to the east and stayed together

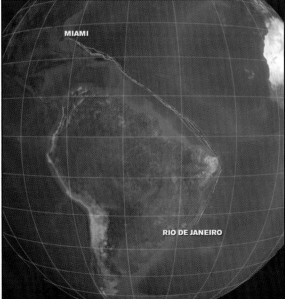

Leg five from Rio de Janeiro to Miami.
Distance 4,450 nautical miles.

as a pack with the exception of *News Corp* who hugged the coast to the west.

SEB and *illbruck* crossed tacks repeatedly over the first few hours. On one tack, *SEB* on port, bore off to pass behind *illbruck* on starboard. *SEB* misjudged the distance and rammed hard into *illbruck's* port quarter. All 24 sailors aboard the two boats were shocked. Gunnar Krantz performed the obligatory 720-degree penalty turn, but Kostecki informed of his intention to protest over the Internet. He felt the 720-degree turn wasn't enough of a penalty considering the damage to his boat: *illbruck* lost her lifelines back aft, suffered a hole, and the integrity of the spinnaker block area was damaged. *SEB* lost a chunk of her bow. Neither skipper would recover psychologically from the incident; Krantz was embarrassed while Kostecki feared a collision like this could put his boat out of commission for an entire leg. Adding to Kostecki's problems, *illbruck* destroyed her Code 0 sail in a separate incident. Ultimately, *illbruck* decided not to protest officially at the conclusion of the race, but in an interesting twist,

SEB rounds the Bahamas for the final run into Miami. Damage to her bow sustained after a collision with illbruck *is visible.*

illbruck, Day Two

I was worried because at this time I could see their bow coming right at us and I thought they would hit us amidships.

Sailing an offshore race of 4,500 miles, you do not need to put your boat in a tight situation such as SEB. This whole incident has slowed us down and will haunt us this entire leg.

John Kostecki

SEB, Day Two

The 720 we had to do after a situation with illbruck *didn't help, but it is really good to be back racing again.*

Gunnar Krantz

djuice, Day Two

Did you see our start? What a gem!

Some of the lads are a bit reluctant to share some of their Brazilian tales yet, but give it a week and I should have quite a bit of gossip to report.

Anthony Nossiter

The gun goes off from the three-masted bark Cisno Branco *signalling the start of leg five as the V.O.60s leave Rio de Janeiro for Miami.* News Corp's *path is nearly blocked by an over-zealous spectator boat.*

the Race Committee protested against *SEB* for "inflicting serious damage to themselves." *SEB* was relieved when the International Jury threw out the protest, which, if upheld, could have cost *SEB* her five points won in leg five.

As the fleet sailed north, the heat intensified. *News Corp* ran out of wind and lost 36 miles in 12 hours. Skipper Jez Fanstone kept to his westerly strategy even though his team dropped from first to seventh.

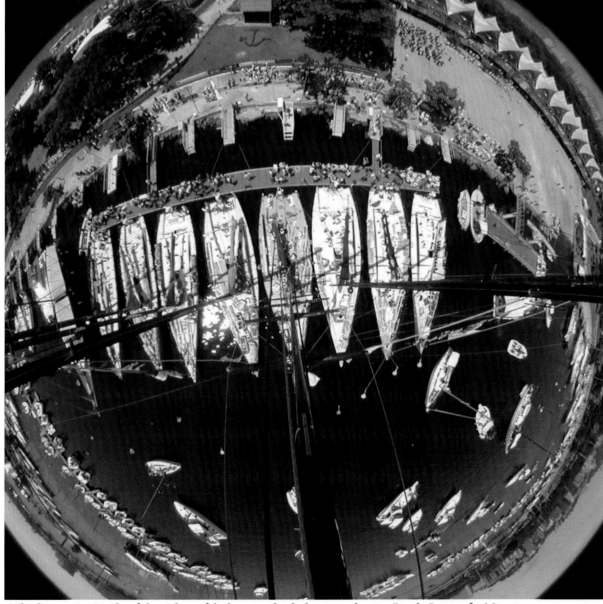

A "bird's eye view" with a fish eye lens of the boats at the dock prior to leaving Rio de Janeiro for Miami.

SEB, Day Five

The bunk I sleep in is known affectionately as "the coffin." Jammed right up between the cockpit side and the face of the aft ballast tank it would be unbearable but for one thing—a ventilation porthole, which lets cool breeze through right onto your face.

On the inside face of the vent someone has added a personal touch, graffiti that says "is this a long race or what?" I laugh every time I see it.

Jon Gundersen

News Corp, Day Four

Life on board is hot and smelly. Twelve sweaty bodies on a 60-foot boat is not a nice smell.

Ross Field

Tyco, *Assa Abloy*, and *illbruck* slowly emerged as the leaders, with close racing as the three boats leap frogged over each other. *illbruck* was no longer dominant as fleet speeds equalized. *Assa Abloy's* Magnus Olsson was jubilant: "We're in a psychological war with *illbruck*. They thought they were sailing like normal, so they passed some boats like they usually do, but now we are actually a little bit faster than them, it's fantastic! I think they are confused. They are behind us and they are getting further and further behind. In these conditions we can actually match their speed. It's really nice."

Kostecki took it all in stride. With a seven-point overall lead staying close was important, and he still had confidence in his all-star crew. Then *Assa Abloy* started luffing *illbruck*. Ray Davies on *illbruck* thought the harassment, 4,000 miles from the finish, was unnecessary: "They've been taking us both out, slowing themselves down, slowing us down and really I

Assa Abloy, Day 14

Although we would like to go faster, the moon is getting fuller every night and the temperature milder. The sailing and the competition don't get much better than this.

Mark Rudiger

Tyco, Day 6

Clouds have been the biggest factor so far as 1 minute you are the peacock and the next minute you're looking like the feather duster.

Jonathon Swain

Assa Abloy, Day 10

Today we were even treated by a visit from a baby killer whale that seemed to enjoy our company as it swam effortlessly alongside her newfound friends.

Jason Carrington

Assa Abloy in second place passing Barbuda in the Caribbean at dawn. For the first time the crew of Assa Abloy was confident it had the boat speed to be competitive against illbruck.

Noel Drennan aboard illbruck about to receive his judgement from King Neptune and Queen Codfish during the first-timers ceremony.

can't see the tactics with four thousand miles to go. It's a bit early for that sort of carry on."

The battle helped all three leaders stretch to a 17-mile lead. What little wind there was could be found under dark clouds. At one point Tyco gained a 7-mile lead only to be snapped right back into the leading pack.

For *djuice* the fast start proved to be an illusion. Knut Frostad reported that their speed was off the pace on "certain angles." *SEB* headed furthest west and was in last on day eight but began to move up with more wind. By day nine *SEB* was in 4th, despite her chipped bow. The top three extended to a 50-mile lead.

At the equator King Neptune provided some

Leg Five Results

Position	Yacht	Elapsed Time	Leg Points	Overall Points	Overall Standings
1	Assa Abloy	17 days 13 hours 19 minutes	8	28	2
2	illbruck	17 days 14 hours 21 minutes	7	36	1
3	Tyco	17 days 14 hours 34 minutes	6	24	4
4	SEB	17 days 17 hours 16 minutes	5	17	7
5	News Corp	17 days 18 hours 26 minutes	4	23	5
6	Amer Sports One	17 days 20 hours 47 minutes	3	25	3
7	djuice	19 days 0 hours 37 minutes	2	19	6
8	Amer Sports Too	19 days 2 hours 33 minutes	1	8	8

comic relief to the heat. No doubt the "first timers" appreciated the humor.

On day 12 *illbruck* was comfortably ahead with a 12-mile lead over *Assa Abloy*. The boats were reaching in the easterly trade winds with no passing lanes: the leaders simply got richer.

A new foe attacked the sailors: flying fish. The silver fish stunk and were a menace, as several sailors were hit in the face. Below deck, life was miserable. The combination of heat and saltwater caused rashes, boils, and chafing.

Spirits lifted two weeks into the race off the eastern Caribbean, with dolphin and whale sightings. The boats, the sailors, the clouds, water and sea life all seemed to exist as one, with great sailing under clear skies and building winds.

The women on *Amer Sports Too* were thrilled as they sailed their best leg to date. They spent a lot of time in sixth place and in contention with the leaders. With the heavy winds of the Southern Ocean behind them, this crew was finally in the game. American Katie Pettibone summed up their feelings: "We're not surprised at how competitive we are. We knew it would take time and practice and here we are."

Day 17 saw action all over the race course: *Assa Abloy* regained second when *Tyco* lost her spinnaker. *djuice* finally passed *Amer Sports Too*, *News Corp* finally passed *Amer Sports One* after a 5-day battle, *Amer Sports One* got hit by lightning and lost all electronics, and *Amer Sports Too* reported problems with pumps, the water maker, and electronics. For the several boats that blew out their spinnakers, the race was now like playing golf without a driver.

With 142 miles left to Miami, *Assa Abloy*, *Tyco*, and *illbruck* all had a chance to win. The breezes disappeared while the powerful Gulf Stream current carried the boats north. It was anyone's race. *Assa Abloy* worked into the Florida coast to escape the current and found a new breeze to arrive first.

Neal McDonald was overjoyed after the 4,450-mile, three-way battle: "It was very, very close. We had a hell of a day fighting it out with *illbruck*."

John Kostecki was a little disappointed but retained a comfortable eight-point margin: "Sailing side by side with *Assa Abloy* and *Tyco*, it was very noticeable that we are similar in speed. They've really copied our sails and a lot of things that we've learned. Now they are catching up so it is going to be a tight race the rest of the way around the world." ▶

Caribbean or Southern Ocean? djuice *finds some weather off the coast of the West Indies. Squalls meant wind, which explains why this crew is smiling during the downpour.*

Assa Abloy *on the podium celebrating their win, first into Miami.*

illbruck, Day Five

Here in the Chesapeake it was tricky. The wind was up and down and shut off at one point for us when we were actually in the lead. News Corp and Amer Sports One did a really nice job of scooting away, and at the same time, Assa Abloy came up behind and passed us. Just tricky wind conditions and we got caught on the wrong side.

John Kostecki

Leg Six
Miami to Baltimore

illbruck after the start of leg six from Miami to Baltimore. Everyone on board is thinking: "What can I do next to improve speed?"

Amer Sports Too, Day Two

We had a plan, a goal to get clear air and a clear lane to race down the beach, time was ticking, hearts were racing, anxiety building, boats were spinning around in close proximity, one eye on the start line—one eye on the clock—one eye on the competition (how many eyes?) and the sail call was crucial, with three on standby—the bow team was ready for anything.

Lisa McDonald

Leg Six
Short Sprint

"Let's get fired up!" was the battle cry of 12 teenage cheerleaders on the deck of *Assa Abloy* departing Miami. The inspiration worked: with 5 minutes to go before the start, *Assa Abloy* attacked *illbruck* match-race style looking for an advantage. Within seconds Chris Larson screamed, "Protest!" alleging that *illbruck* had sailed outside the spectator exclusion zone. As a guest aboard *Assa Abloy* with a great view of the action, it was apparent to me that *illbruck's* helmsman John Kostecki was annoyed by *Assa Abloy's* aggression: *Assa Abloy's* Magnus Olsson had said before the start that his team had to defeat *illbruck* on this leg to have any chance of winning the overall prize—in the end, *Assa Abloy* never did file the protest.

The two boats ended up head to wind while the rest of the fleet locked horns battling for the heavily favored port end of the start line. Thirty seconds before the gun, *Assa Abloy* was stuck in irons frantically trying to recover. Kostecki had quickly turned the tables. The great thing in sailing, however, is that changes are inevitable. *Assa Abloy's* fortunes looked

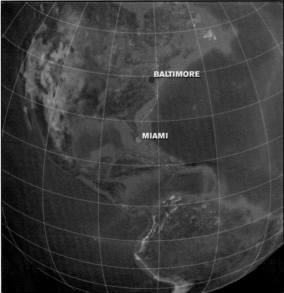

dismal trailing the fleet as the gun fired. But a miracle occurred: six boats, including *illbruck*, had jumped the gun. Unlike the 100-yard dash, in sailing only the offending boats need to return to the starting line, giving a huge advantage to the yachts who started correctly. There was lots of confusion as the six boats took down spinnakers and circled back to start correctly, while *Amer Sports Too* and *Assa Abloy*, who made clean starts, surged into the lead.

Surprisingly, on the second day *Amer Sports Too* split with the fleet and headed east, separating from the pack by 50 miles. It took a while but *illbruck* passed *Assa Abloy* on that day. For *Tyco* there was a brief recovery but bad luck haunted the boat. One could feel the frustration on board. Navigator Steve Hayles wrote the following e-mail: "This leg will stick in our memory for a long time. The bad cloud on the morning of the second day was just the start of it. At

Leg six from Miami to Baltimore. Distance 875 nautical miles.

every turn things have conspired to make the race difficult. We've been battling in literally no wind for several hours. The boats behind are rolling into us. The boats ahead have extended their leads. We were right next to *SEB* a day ago, but now they are miles ahead." Throughout day two every boat made multiple sail changes while desperately trying to gain an edge. *Assa Abloy*, *illbruck*, *News Corp*, and *Amer Sports One* stretched into a nice lead. At one point *Assa Abloy* had to stop the boat and put a man over the side to clear seaweed off the rudder.

Two-time Olympic gold medalist Mark Reynolds was invited onboard *SEB* for leg six. After 2 days he joked, "In the last 2 days I guess I've gotten in more sailing than I normally do in a whole year. I used to think that hiking out was hard. But moving these sails all around, in and out, and up and down is a lot more work than sailing a Star boat in an hour-and-a-half race."

At Cape Fear the wind went light, only 5 knots and very fluky. *News Corp* took the lead for the first time, and the top four boats traded positions frequently. The racing was tense and the crews were weary after making endless sail changes.

The women on *Amer Sports Too* fell behind as a result of their junket to the east, although they did rally and ended up close to *djuice*, *Tyco*, and *SEB*. The ever-optimistic Lisa McDonald was happy that her team was finally sailing at the level of the other boats.

As dawn broke on day four, *News Corp*, with *Amer Sports One* close behind, passed through the Lucius J. Kellam Bridge/Tunnel. The flat water was a welcome relief for the wide, flat-bottomed *Amer Sports One*. As the fleet sailed north into the Chesapeake, Grant Dalton and his crew closed on *News Corp*, and finally passed at noon. Aboard *News Corp* skipper Jez Fanstone was not about to give up.

Assa Abloy, Day Three

We picked up a load of weed on the keel, strut, and rudder. We tried to floss it off but finally had to stop and Richard dove in to pull it off. This we had to do twice! Then after working ahead again, yours truly accidentally hit the wrong switch in the dark with the generator running and exploded a ballast line and almost sank the boat!

Mark Rudiger

SEB, Day Two

We started making sail changes, putting up different sails one right after the other, sometimes only minutes apart. At first I just thought that the boys wanted to show me all the nice sails they had but after they all had been up once we started going through them once again. Despite how much trouble these sails are, they make the boat go fast and I actually slept next to one last night. I guess it's a love hate relationship.

Mark Reynolds

djuice **after the start of leg six from Miami to Baltimore. Knut Frostad sailed with 22 different people over nine legs.**

News Corp, Day Four

Everyone on board is at the height of concentration, coiled springs ready to do whatever to make a gain or save a boat length. I don't think I have ever been in a more intense yacht race.

Jez Fanstone

The view from News Corp must have been intimidating after jumping the gun at the start and being last to restart. Before they finished the crew would work their boat into the lead.

Over 100,000 people visited Baltimore's Inner Harbor on Saturday, April 20, 2002, after the fleet's arrival.

The level of intensity aboard the boats was impressive. Most Bay sailors would give up in such light conditions, but the V.O.60s sailed at 7 knots in 7 knots of wind.

Grant Dalton and crew welcomed the fluky conditions because they felt *Amer Sports One* would excel. At 1:30 in the afternoon, *News Corp* and *Amer Sports One* stopped dead in the water one boatlength apart. Both crews looked like ballet dancers as they moved about the deck changing sails. *News Corp* was the first to gain some momentum. The crew of *Amer Sports One* looked stunned as *News Corp* slowly sailed over the top only a few feet away.

News Corp worked the west side of Chesapeake Bay

Amer Sports Too **sails toward the finish line at the end of leg six from Miami to Baltimore.**

Leg Six Results

Position	Yacht	Elapsed Time	Leg Points	Overall Points	Overall Standings
1	News Corp	3 days 13 hours 12 minutes	8	31	4
2	Amer Sports One	3 days 13 hours 38 minutes	7	32	3
3	Assa Abloy	3 days 13 hours 58 minutes	6	34	2
4	illbruck	3 days 14 hours 1 minute	5	41	1
5	SEB	3 days 21 hours 42 minutes	4	21	6
6	Tyco	4 days 1 hour 0 minutes	3	27	5
7	djuice	4 days 1 hour 10 minutes	2	21	7
8	Amer Sports Too	4 days 1 hour 46 minutes	1	9	8

Alby (Alistair) Pratt at the helm of News Corp *with Ian Walker trimming.* Amer Sports One *is in hot pursuit. Having another boat so close keeps the pressure on.*

while the other three boats all favored the east. The wind filled from the west. *News Corp* continued to gain and would hold the lead all the way to the finish.

The Race Committee had the option of finishing the boats at the Bay Bridge off Annapolis or sailing all the way to Fort McHenry at the entrance to Baltimore's Inner Harbor. At 10 p.m. the Race Committee decided the fleet would sail all the way to Baltimore.

A northwest breeze slowly drifted across the fleet but it was hard work and agonizingly slow. *News Corp* had to deal with a departing ship and barge in the narrow channel. The pilot aboard the tug later complimented *News Corp's* Damien (Shreda) Duke who was awarded the Sjoo Sandstrom Seamanship Award for his skill in averting a potentially dangerous situation.

Further back, *Tyco, djuice,* and *Amer Sports Too* were also having a tight race. For the first time the women on *Amer Sports Too* had a realistic chance of beating another boat to the finish line. They finished 50 minutes behind *Tyco* and 40 minutes behind *djuice.*

The cities of Baltimore and Annapolis welcomed the Volvo Ocean Race fleet with open arms during an 11-day extravaganza. On the Saturday after the boats arrived, over 100,000 people flocked to Baltimore's impressive Inner Harbor to see the race boats, treating the sailors as heroes. 🚩

It feels all right! Fantastic! Three years work for me and months and years for all the crew. A huge team effort, fantastic.

Jez Fanstone, News Corp

Congratulations to News Corp *and Jez, they sailed a very good leg. It's getting pretty busy at the top now, but it is certainly competitive, and we are just pleased to be here and have a good lead, as we sailed really well.*

Grant Dalton, Amer Sports One

It was particularly tough out there. The Chesapeake Bay proved to be exactly what we thought it would be. Light, difficult, and opportunities to gain and lose a lot. We made the gains we needed to in the last 20 hours of the race.

Neal McDonald, Assa Abloy

Team News Corp *at the prize giving at Baltimore after winning leg six from Miami to Baltimore.*

Assa Abloy, Day Five

From a very wet Assa Abloy. We are back into fire hose reaching mode after a brief relief this morning. We are racing along blast reaching, chasing illbruck as hard as we can.

Richard Mason

Leg Seven
Annapolis to La Rochelle

Assa Abloy *finished second in leg seven from Annapolis to La Rochelle.*

Amer Sports One, Day 10

It is exactly a year ago that the first crewmembers arrived in La Ciotat, France, to help finish building the boats.
Only one year . . . time flies.

Bouwe Bekking

Leg Seven
World Record Set

After 27,975 miles of racing, the Baltimore–Annapolis stopover was a great time to sit down and interview all eight skippers. Even though they had been at it for 7 months, one third of the points were still up for grabs, and the race was heavy on everyone's mind.

illbruck—Mentally it can be a struggle at times but we have a great crew, and that winning attitude. So it's pretty easy for us. I really believe you are not pushing the boat hard enough unless you broach once or twice during the leg. If you throttle back you're not going to win the race so you've got to keep pushing all the way. We have good experienced guys on board and we're making the best calls we can make at the time. You have to keep going and not let up. —**John Kostecki**

Assa Abloy—I think we've got as much chance as anybody. It won't take an awful lot to make it quite difficult for them to stay ahead of whomever is in second. One attribute that I bring in as a skipper is I see the receiving end of any decisions made quite clearly because most of my sailing career has been not as a skipper. —**Neal McDonald**

Amer Sports One—The harder it blows the more you've got to throttle it down because you can make quite good gains in that stuff. If we don't stand on the podium in every leg pretty much we won't even retain third let alone get up to second and challenge for first. —**Grant Dalton**

News Corp—We're ultimately a speed-based sport and it is run on adrenaline. If you have a lot of adrenaline you drive the boat really hard and you go fast. But if you drive it too hard you crash and go slow. If you're too fearful you drive the boat too slow and you lose miles as well. —**Jez Fanstone**

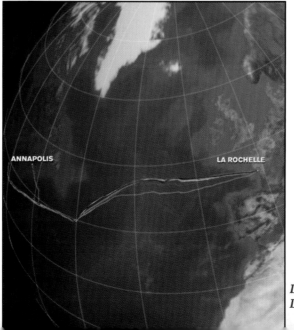

ANNAPOLIS   **LA ROCHELLE**

Tyco—We've got a lot of belief in ourselves really and we set realistic goals for ourselves after we broke the rudder. We want a podium finish. —**Kevin Shoebridge**

SEB—We can theoretically get up in the top three but we need to get on the podium on the next leg. And then from there we see how far we can get. If you don't give back to the sponsors what they've invested for, you don't have a job next time. —**Gunnar Krantz**

djuice—We are up and down and it's a very close fleet. There's only good boats. Finishing sixth in a fleet like this is a hopeless position . . . if there were 25 boats and only six good boats it would look a lot better. —**Knut Frostad**

Amer Sports Too—Look at who we are actually racing against. We're racing against guys that have done this race five, six, seven times more than we have. I think each leg we're definitely getting better and more confident.—**Lisa McDonald**

With a tornado off Sydney still vividly in the memory of the Volvo Ocean Race competitors, the forecast of possible tornadoes crossing the racecourse on Chesapeake Bay loomed large. Pouring rain, dark skies, and a building breeze greeted the sailors as they boarded their yachts docked at Annapolis' historic waterfront. One could sense this would be a challenging day.

Leg seven from Annapolis to La Rochelle.
Distance 3,400 nautical miles.

The starting line was set just north of the 4-mile-long Chesapeake Bay Bridge, with the area lined by a corridor of 1,200 hearty boats. The famous schooner, *Pride of Baltimore II*, sat majestically on the starting line. Small-boat ace Gavin Brady engineered a perfect start for *SEB*, and with an ebb tide, the fleet made a swift exit under the Bay Bridge. At one point, all eight boats sailed simultaneously between the twin spans. It was an impressive sight.

Tactician Dee Smith on *Amer Sports One* maneuvered his boat into the lead as the fleet passed through a gate near Thomas Point Lighthouse. Overall race leader *illbruck* was well back at this point.

Later that night a devastating tornado ripped apart the town of LaPlata, Maryland. Luckily the V.O.60s were 50 miles away and safely out of the deadly spout's reach. Once out in the open ocean, the first challenge was to find the Gulf Stream flowing toward Europe, which would give each boat a free couple of miles each hour. Despite her slow start, *illbruck* was first into the Stream.

Amer Sports Too, Day Four

Beautiful day for downwind sailing. The breeze is steady in strength and the current is running strong, wooshing us toward the middle of the ocean.

Lisa McDonald

A powerful northwest breeze pushed the fleet hard. *illbruck* reported hitting a remarkable 29.9 knots, and on day three they set a new 24-hour record sailing 473 miles. *djuice* blew out a critical spinnaker and *SEB's* Code 6 blew apart.

Then *illbruck* set another new record of 484 miles in 24 hours, thanks to 25 to 30 knots of wind harnessed with a masthead spinnaker. The boat surfed down large waves and was carried toward the northeast in the 3 to 4-knot Gulf Steam current. There was speculation that the record should not count but the World Sailing Speed Record Council was quick to point out that there are currents all over the world and the record would stand. John Kostecki was ecstatic, "All in all I'm

SEB, Day Five

Again, we all had the same chance of being where illbruck was and had the same chance to break the record on this leg. They did it and good on them.

Gunnar Krantz

Thanks to heavy wind and a boost from the Gulf Stream, illbruck *set a new world record for a monohull yacht of 484 nautical miles in 24 hours during leg seven.*

just really happy about it, really proud of everybody onboard the boat. Everybody pushed hard and it's a great achievement."

On the same day *Amer Sports Too* broke her mast 30 feet off the deck in only 15 knots of wind. Liz Wardley summed up the attitude on board, "You look up and it's the most depressing, unbelievable thing that can happen to you in a yacht race. She went, just like that. It's unbe-

djuice, Day 11

I am so tired of freeze-dried food that it is above description. I blatantly refuse to eat the rice and curry. . . Give any convict a few days on rice and curry and they will confess to whatever you want them to confess. I hereby confess that I am looking forward to the French cuisine. The whole lot of it. They can throw anything on my plate and I will kiss their feet.

Stig Westergaard

lievable, you don't know what to think. You just duck and hope it doesn't land on your head."

Amer Sports Too was towed all the way into Halifax by the Canadian Coast Guard icebreaker *Edward Cornwallis*. The crippled boat just made it into port in a gale with wind speeds of 58 knots, and treacherous seas for a boat under tow. While the rest of the fleet raced toward Europe, the disappointed *Amer Sports*

illbruck, Day 12

It was tricky from the beginning, going down the Chesapeake Bay, a big difference could have potentially happened there, and it was also very tricky going around the Gulf Stream—not to miss the Gulf Stream. We managed to do that well and sail the boat fast, we had good sails and our inventory that we took for this leg worked very, very well—I think that is why we ended up with the big difference.

Juan Vila

The fleet of V.O.60s maneuver under the Bay Bridge after the start of leg seven. The annual bridge walk was cancelled due to thunderstorms. Four years earlier the fleet sailed under this bridge to the roar of 50,000 fans.

The fleet lined up in La Rochelle at the end of leg seven.

Too fought to get their boat shipped to Europe, repaired, and ready on the starting line for leg eight.

djuice, Day Three

Yesterday evening, our favorite heavy air spinnaker, the fractional Code 5, exploded into three pieces. It has been a catastrophe for us, as this has been the right sail to have up ever since it broke.

Knut Frostad

illbruck, Day Five

It would be fine if at the end of a big day you could drop sails and motor home but it just goes on.

Mark Christensen

The other sailors were fatigued from sailing in high speeds and constantly changing sails. Most of the boats stayed close together, forced to make a pre-set mark mid-ocean that was designed to keep the fleet away from the ice to the north. The weather ahead presented a strategic quandary. High pressure to the south contrasted with powerful 40-knot winds to the north,

A quiet spot in the weather so the News Corp *team hog some tasty freeze-dried food, left to right: Damion Duke, Stuart Childerley, skipper Jez Fanstone and Matt Humphries.*

offering a tricky balance between sailing the rhumb line looking for wind and riding the Stream. Frustratingly, the windier it got, the slower *Amer Sports One* seemed to sail compared with the fleet. Grant Dalton wrote by e-mail about the problems in sailing his "fat, flat-bottomed boat."

Meanwhile Gavin Brady on *SEB* thrived on the heavy-wind sailing, "Surfing down waves at 30 knots and pushing the boat to a level that is just crazy is what this race is all about. We were sailing as hard as we could and just waiting for the boat to spin out of control or break. I was down below when the boat suddenly rounded up going 25 knots. The Code 6 spinnaker blew out. This was a big problem. It took 12 hours to repair the damage."

SEB, Day Nine

It's a nervous time here on SEB *as we find out whether our breakaway move from the pack is going to pay dividends. All fingers are crossed here.*

Gareth Cooke

illbruck continued to extend her lead to 28 miles after the first week. At this point *SEB* split with the fleet and took a bold flier south, but *illbruck* wisely elected to cover *Assa Abloy* and leave *SEB* alone. Initially *SEB* took a loss, but hoping for a long-term gain Gunnar Krantz maintained his course. Crews reported a lot of problems with gear as the heavy wind took its toll.

Aboard *illbruck* the stomach flu slammed the crew in a cruel turn of fate. *SEB* in the south moved into fourth while *Amer Sports One* and *News Corp* battled one mile apart. Gordon Maguire, aboard *News Corp*, said, "It's all gone from fast and furious to fickle and light so it's going to be quite interesting to see what's going to happen. *SEB* and ourselves are the southernmost boats in the fleet at the moment and I guess we're feeling a little bit exposed."

For *djuice* it was more bad news. It seemed that Knut Frostad simply could not get a break. "Twice now weird things have happened because the wind has just

Amer Sports Too *through the fog as the Canadian Coast Guard ice breaker,* Edward Cornwallis, *took the V.O.60 in tow because of a broken mast and deteriorating weather conditions 200 nautical miles off Halifax.*

shut down for us only. Don't ask me? Sometimes you wonder when you are getting nailed, again, and again, and again. So I wonder what I have done to deserve this. The only leg so far that we didn't park up at all was leg four but we can come back, and we will."

The lighter winds lined up a parade to the finish. Carrying a bigger sail, *Amer Sports One* passed *News Corp*, a dramatic moment avenging *News Corp's* passing *Amer Sports One* in Chesapeake Bay on leg six.

Grant Dalton kept looking ahead, "We certainly didn't place the boat very well. But our speed is okay. Let's hope we can get through." *News Corp's* Jez Fanstone was unfazed at this point, "Every time we get ahead, something happens and they manage to

Leg Seven Results

Position	Yacht	Elapsed Time	Leg Points	Overall Points	Overall Standings
1	illbruck	10 days 20 hours 44 minutes	8	49	1
2	AssaAbloy	10 days 23 hours 39 minutes	7	41	2
3	Tyco	11 days 0 hours 19 minutes	6	33	5
4	SEB	11 days 1 hour 53 minutes	5	26	6
5	Amer Sports One	11 days 2 hours 4 minutes	4	36	3
6	News Corp	11 days 2 hours 42 minutes	3	34	4
7	djuice	11 days 8 hours 9 minutes	2	23	7
8	Amer Sports Too	Retired from leg	1	10	8

come back again. As long as they finish behind us, we don't mind." Gavin Brady on *SEB* observed that late in the race, sailors always seem to become defensive, working mainly to hold their position, and that these moves are not always smart.

John Kostecki was nervous, but he and his team held on, with *illbruck* finishing 37 miles ahead of *Assa Abloy*. Tyco finished third—for the fourth time. Meanwhile *SEB's* bold move south earned her a fourth-place finish. ⛵

We are still pretty happy to be here in third, especially with News Corp *back in sixth. Hopefully* SEB *will do the job on Dalts (*Amer Sports One*) and then the whole thing is on again.*

Kevin Shoebridge, Tyco

About 7 days ago we hit something, doing about 15 knots, just as it was becoming daylight and we couldn't see what was going on and the boat started going slowly and quite sluggish so we dropped the spinnaker and did a back down, rehoisted and got going again. It wasn't until a few days later that we started having suspicions. We were not sure until Nigel dove over the side as we finished just to see, and we have lost the bottom six inches of the rudder. We were just struggling for pace.

Jez Fanstone, News Corp

Amer Sports One *motored into the ancient port of La Rochelle.*

illbruck's *crew looks relieved after winning leg seven.*

Leg Eight
La Rochelle to Göteborg

News Corp, Day Two

What a battle . . . the fleet within a few miles of each other rounding the notorious Ushant, traveling at 20 knots in 30 knots of wind blowing from the west. We have had a tight race since the start and we are soaking wet after a slog to this left-hand corner. Very unpleasant conditions have resulted in some of the crew spending time on the white telephone to god.

Matthew Humphries

News Corp *and* illbruck *close to Ushant. Blast reaching is hard work for the helmsman. Rotation takes place every 30 minutes.*

Assa Abloy, Day Three

So it's full throttle and all the coal to the burners aboard Assa Abloy. *We need to fight it out for a few more days so we can be the first to see the motherland.*

Mark Rudiger

Leg Eight
Currents, Shallows, and Rocks

With two legs remaining in the Volvo Ocean Race, the final standings were very much in question. Leg eight looked daunting to the navigators: while the length was relatively short at 1,075 miles, there were 27 marks of the course to pass. The fleet would be racing through the crowded Dover Straits and the complex North Sea. Both featured a myriad of obstacles ranging from shipping traffic and oil rigs to shallow spots.

In 18 knots of wind *Amer Sports One* took an early lead, repeating the pattern set by Grant Dalton at the start of leg seven in Annapolis. Clearly *Amer Sports One* liked sailing upwind in a strong breeze.

Assa Abloy found herself early for the starting line. She took a dive to leeward to use up time but ended up to leeward of the layline and snagged the starting buoy. It was an awful mistake. The anchor and buoy dragged behind the boat, taking 8 minutes to get clear. Richard Mason and Jason Carrington had to jump in the water to clear away the buoy and the anchor line, and by the time they got free, they were well over a mile behind the fleet. Morale must have been low on board. Mason summed up the incident succinctly: "Disappointing to have that happen. Disaster."

Several hours later the fleet arranged itself in the usual order with *illbruck* leading followed by *Assa Abloy*, *Tyco*, *News Corp*, and *Amer Sports One*. Both *djuice* and *Amer Sports Too* were off the pace and quickly fell behind. Aboard *Tyco*, Guy Salter injured his leg, meaning the boat would be sailing with a man down.

At one point after the start *djuice* was ahead of *Assa*

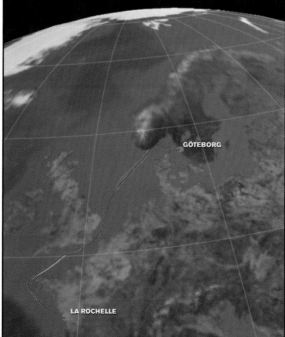

Leg eight from La Rochelle to Göteborg.
Distance 1,075 nautical miles.

Abloy. Knut Frostad reported that *Assa Abloy* passed them like a train, even though *djuice* had everyone on the rail along with every piece of equipment possible on the stack. It was a visual confirmation that *djuice* simply lacked speed.

djuice, Day Two

Assa Abloy *passed us earlier this night on pure speed with less people on deck, looking quite relaxed. We can only remind ourselves that we would have been further back if we hadn't pushed so hard. As we only have two to three guys down below at a time, the bunks are filled with spinnakers. We are just stacked to the limits.*

Knut Frostad

It was a very rough first night with the wind blowing 40 knots. The boats took a vicious pounding as they sailed upwind, and many crew suffered from seasickness. *Amer Sports One* was the first boat to Ushant with a 2-mile lead, but the next five boats were all within 5 miles. The ride was exhilarating as they averaged 19 knots.

Tyco, Day Four

Lets hope it is downwind, 14 to 20 knots with a nice little wave to help boats that surf early, it's not a lot to ask for, is it?

Kevin Shoebridge

Assa Abloy took the southerly route through the English Channel while *Amer Sports One* took the middle road. This allowed *Assa Abloy* to grab the lead with *Tyco* and *Amer Sports One* only one mile behind. The dark cloud following *SEB* around the world continued as *SEB* lost its instruments.

A tactical battle raged as the sailors searched for the best sailing angle and strongest current. *Assa Abloy's* brain trust—McDonald, Larson, and Rudiger—called it right, which must have been quite a relief for the crew of *Assa Abloy* after her slow start. The women aboard *Amer Sports Too*, however, decided to play the English coast to the north and were now 100 miles behind, proving once again that splitting with the fleet did not work.

An Assa Abloy *crew member waves the French national flag from the shrouds as the fleet leaves La Rochelle harbor for the restart of leg eight.*

Concentration levels run high on board Amer Sports One *as she takes a small lead at the start.*

illbruck, Day Four

My biggest goof ups so far have come in the food department . . . still can't quite figure out what time it is to eat. I have now been accused of eating an entire watch's ration of Mars bars (very bad). Not wanting to offend anyone (and being quite fond of chocolate), I have been gladly accepting any bar that was offered. What I did not realize is that sharing treats is proper boat etiquette (that is why they were offered), but you're supposed to politely decline the offer if you have already eaten your daily ration.

Ed Adams

At the front, the first six boats were all within 2 miles of each other, with the leaders changing places frequently. At one point *Tyco* and *SEB* shared the lead.

Many of the lead changes were a result of the race boats backing down to clear seaweed and fish off their keels. If the backdown didn't work, someone had to jump in the water to cut away the flotsam. The backdown could cost over a mile, but it was absolutely necessary to go through this procedure.

SEB, Day Four

Honestly, it seems to work better without the instruments. We sailed really well with just the boat speed and heading on the instruments. As soon as we got some of the numbers back, things started to go wrong and we went from first to fifth place in three hours.

Gunnar Krantz

On the fourth day the fleet was well ahead of schedule. *Assa Abloy* regained the lead with *illbruck* and *Tyco*

Amer Sports Too, Day Three

Amazing conditions, it was an absolute hate mission yesterday heading up to Ushant. The boat was literally sending herself off the top of the waves and thundering down into the crevice beneath, with an almighty shudder as our much-treasured rig twanged and vibrated around up there, sails fully inverted and reverted from the shock, and on deck, one more chick hanging over the side wishing she were anywhere but here, getting beaten up and shaken around like a martini.

Emma Westmacott

The crew of Amer Sports Too *was plagued by illness on leg eight. Nine of 13 were reportedly sick.*

Overhead view of the Volvo village in La Rochelle.

one mile back. *SEB* made a bold move to the north and at one point surged into second but started to lose ground as the fleet headed for Arendal Light off Norway, dodging trawlers and rocks along the way. Aboard *Assa Abloy* a flapping spinnaker sheet removed part of the wheel and Mikey Joubert was hit in the head with a spinnaker shackle. The annoying backdowns to clear seaweed continued throughout the day.

At Skagen Light the fleet essentially had a restart, because the leg was still available to any of the top five

The fleet at the start of leg eight.

boats at this point. They were all within 2 miles of each other. *Assa Abloy* and *Amer Sports One* aggressively played the sandbars trying to gain out of the current. Grant Dalton reported making 47 tacks in 25 knots of wind.

In the most thrilling finish in the history of round-the-world racing, *Assa Abloy* prevailed, followed closely by *Tyco, News Corp, illbruck,* and *Amer Sports One.* The top five boats crossed the finish line in a remarkable 6 minute and 50 second period! *Assa Abloy's* Neal McDonald credited new sails and Mark Rudiger's bril-

Tyco, Day Three

After going slowly for a short while we decided that we had to clear it [the weed] off, which meant hoisting headsail and dropping the spinnaker before rounding up head to wind and going backward.

Brad Jackson

race—we'll go into a normal watch system, sail hard but conserve energy' and I'm sure that paid off. At the end we put the energy where we needed it. We had everyone up for 15 to 16 hours on the rail. By that stage we still had the energy to do that. I think if we'd

liant decisions for their success. Significantly, going into the final leg *Assa Abloy* was now mathematically in a position to win the overall title.

Neal McDonald explained after the race how he was able to stage the comeback: "On the first night we didn't sit it out all night. We said, 'It's a long

Amer Sports One, Day Three

We will see, all the boats are sailing very well and the race is close and fun. Wish all the legs were like this. Stay tuned, anything can happen.

Dee Smith

Leg Eight Results

Position	Yacht	Elapsed Time	Leg Points	Overall Points	Overall Standings
1	Assa Abloy	4 days 7 hours 6 minutes	8	49	2
2	Tyco	4 days 7 hours 8 minutes	7	40	3
3	News Corp	4 days 7 hours 10 minutes	6	40	3
4	illbruck	4 days 7 hours 11 minutes	5	54	1
5	Amer Sports One	4 days 7 hours 13 minutes	4	40	3
6	SEB	4 days 7 hours 57 minutes	3	29	6
7	djuice	4 days 10 hours 19 minutes	2	25	7
8	Amer Sports Too	4 days 18 hours 50 minutes	1	11	8

done that on the first night we wouldn't. Before the start we highlighted what we called hotspots of the race and put our energy into those."

McDonald was also pleased by the new sails they had on board for the leg. "The one thing that we're over the moon about is the new sails developed for this leg, they are incredibly fast. We're a rocket ship upwind and we haven't had that luxury before. Upwind we were blitzing the others."

In an odd twist of fate, *Assa Abloy's* sailing crew and their shore crew had a bet that if the boat finished first, the shore crew was to shave their heads. But if *Assa Abloy* finished second or worse, the sailors would be getting a haircut. True to their word, the shore crew went to the barbershop.

A despondent John Kostecki reported sailhandling problems and tactical errors as the reason for their fourth-place finish. "We made some tactical blunders," admitted Kostecki, showing the pressure of being the leader to that point. "Everyone is really tired, but it's tough to be perfect all the time." With one leg to go, *illbruck* still enjoyed a five-point advantage.

The race for third overall between *Tyco*, *News Corp*, and *Amer Sports One* ended leg eight dramatically with the three boats tied, having 40 points each. 🏴

Assa Abloy, Day Five

What a day. Holy cow. You could cut the tension with a knife and I might even resort to a little drinking after this one. Magnus (Olsson) is running around like a cat on a hot tin roof trying to make up his mind which way to go. Yesterday when SEB was ahead for a little while, we had to sedate him and lash him in his bunk. Klabbe [Klas Nylof] is keeping his cool, but his eyes show an intensity that is a sure sign of an explosion waiting to go off. The rest of us aren't much better, after doing about 55 tacks up the Norwegian coast leaving a track on the GPS plotter that looks more like a saw blade, with little dots marking rocks all around.

Mark Rudiger

Enjoying downwind sailing on Assa Abloy. This crew is in the groove.

Skipper Neal MacDonald and his crew from Assa Abloy receive first prize for leg eight. They are as jubilant as a winning football team.

Leg Nine
Göteborg to Kiel

Amer Sports One, Day Two

Five minutes ago we rounded Kiel lighthouse. Only nine miles to the finish of this last sprint from Göteborg. At this moment we are lucky to have Tyco and News Corp behind.

Roger Nilson

News Corp, Tyco *and* Amer Sports One *leave Göteborg on leg nine, each striving for third place overall. The spectator boats made the departure difficult, but the sailors did not seem to notice. They were only focused on each other.*

djuice, Day Two

We have waited so long for this, and tried and tried and tried so hard. Never have we been lighter and faster, and probably never sailed better. I haven't slept since Göteborg, but does it really matter? Göteborg had the best start. Kiel had the best finish. That's what we think, anyway.

Knut Frostad

Leg Nine
The Final Moment

Amazingly, the final positions for seven of the eight boats were still in question at the start of the final leg. The people of Göteborg turned out en mass. Veteran round-the-world sailors Gunnar Krantz and Mark Rudiger reported that there were more people in boats than they had ever seen at a sailing event. It had been a terrific stopover in Volvo's hometown.

Unfortunately, the wind was light for the start. *illbruck's* John Kostecki went for an aggressive start and won it. His mission was to stay close to *Assa Abloy*. For its part *Assa Abloy* still had a mathematical chance to win the whole thing if she could be first into Kiel and somehow get *illbruck* back to sixth. Sailors understand in light winds anything can happen, and that kept hopes alive.

illbruck, Day Two

Tracking Assa Abloy is a full-time job, essential because our only tactic this race is to cover them no matter where they go. Every five minutes we log her range and bearing and analyze the relative gain or loss.

Ed Adams

For sailing fans Göteborg provided a festival atmosphere. But for *Tyco*, *Amer Sports One*, and *News Corp* (all tied for third place) this 250-mile leg would prove to be intense. America's Cup navigator Peter Isler returned to sail aboard *News Corp*. Grant Dalton, on *Amer Sports One*, had a podium finish in all of his previous six round-the-world races and did

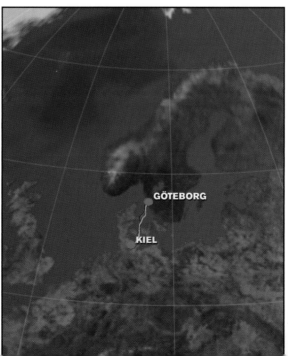

Leg nine from Göteborg to Kiel. Distance 250 nautical miles.

not want to break his successful record. *Tyco* had momentum on her side after the disappointment of breaking her rudder on leg two.

The battle for sixth was still undecided. If *djuice* could somehow win and *SEB* finish sixth, *djuice* would move up a place in the overall standings. The women were frustrated at being last to finish on every leg and they hoped that light wind on the short leg would be to their advantage.

With all these scenarios in mind every competitor was focused in a way rarely seen during a light wind start. *News Corp* dropped two crew to save weight. Knut Frostad went a step further and dropped three crew off his boat to save weight. It was the first time any boat sailed shorthanded in the Volvo Ocean Race. Frostad also debuted a new huge Code 0 sail. Frostad was hungry in spite of all the adversity *djuice* had suffered over the last 9 months.

Assa Abloy nearly collided with a spectator boat soon after the start. The wind was out of the east at 8 to 12 knots but very patchy. With the narrow channel crowded with at least 2,000 spectator boats, undisturbed wind was hard to find. The fleet had to jibe frequently to stay clear. There was a real premium on smooth sailhandling.

SEB, Day Two

I have never before seen so many spectators on the water. A solid wall that affected the wind is what we saw behind and around us after the start.

Gunnar Krantz

News Corp, Day One

All of us on News Corp *want to thank the people of Göteborg for such a great send off. If any port deserved a stopover they did.*

Matt Humphries

Tyco, Day One

A really difficult start though with very light and fluky conditions as a sea breeze fought hard with the gradient wind from the east, which left us all parked at times. We are now as a fleet on our way south to Kiel and ironically on the shortest leg of the race by a long way we have already got the biggest split we have ever seen after only a few hours racing.

It will be many hours before we have any idea who is right and who is wrong.

Steve Hayles

By four in the afternoon, the fleet split into two groups. The big decision facing the teams was which way to pass Anholt Island. *Tyco, SEB,* and *News Corp* elected to sail west of the island. The other five boats took the eastern route. "The wind had gone through nearly 360 degrees twice, gone completely calm three times, the waypoint list is over 50 long, and there have been big islands and small shoals lying on the rhumb-line (with the fleet split as to which way to go around them)," said Ed Adams, of *illbruck.*

illbruck **sails under Stora Belt Bridge.**

Surprisingly, *djuice* was doing well. Knut Frostad took some chances sailing over the sandbanks on the east side of the island of Anholt, and reported a half knot of favorable current in the shallow water.

Around midnight, *Tyco, SEB,* and *News Corp* ended up anchored to keep from drifting backward in a strong, unfavorable current. Over the next 4 hours this trio would lose 20 miles to the easterly boats. "For 2 hours we battled a knot and a quarter of foul tide without enough wind to make forward progress—anchored firmly in the mud. *SEB* and *Tyco* were nearby and anchored too. But the group to the east never stopped, and that put us where we are now . . . hoping for another parking lot to even things out," said Peter Isler on *News Corp.*

Göteborg, Sweden. The huge crowds line the headlands at the start of leg nine.

A crew member aboard Amer Sports One *at the top of the mast looking for wind. In light air this was a standard technique.*

Göteborg, Sweden. June 5, 2002. Parade of Sail on the Göte River.

djuice, Day One

Passing the sandbanks on the east side of Anholt was quite scary. We went as close as we dared to, but I had three different charts showing depths varying from 3.7 to 5.5 meters where we went. We ended up trusting the German charts, and they seemed to be right in the end as we skirted over 4.2 meters depth giving as much as a foot of water under the bulb [of the keel].

Knut Frostad

Assa Abloy's Neal McDonald was amazed as *djuice* sailed past, leaving *illbruck* in second, *Assa Abloy* third, and *Amer Sports One* fourth. *djuice's* new sail and light weight clearly made a difference. In another surprise, *Amer Sports Too* was close behind.

By 10 the next morning *djuice* was off Langland Island, Denmark, and only 40 miles from the finish. The wind freshened out of the east. With *News Corp* and *Tyco* still stuck in light air, *Amer Sports One* seemed assured of a third overall. But in a new twist their stablemate, *Amer Sports Too*, passed them. Dalton had said in the 1997–98 Whitbread Race that if he lost to the women he would run up Auckland's Queen Street nude with a pineapple in a very uncomfortable place. There was a lot of "pineapple" talk aboard *Amer Sports Too*.

The Volvo Ocean Race Committee decided to shorten the course so the leading boats would finish in daylight. A huge crowd was waiting for the sailors. Again there were reports that the arrival fleet was bigger than anyone could remember, with hundreds of boats on the water, and 250,000 people on land. The wind died and the boats ghosted across the finish line. *djuice* was first. Knut Frostad appeared to be somewhere between elated and ecstatic: "This has to be the best moment in my life. To finish the race on such a high note. For the first time this race I feel really happy. It's a bit hard to describe how I feel at the moment, how this affects everyone on the team and our sponsors. To see the smiles on the faces of the sponsors in the spectator boats as we crossed the line was just amazing. To know that we haven't let everybody down entirely is just so good."

Frostad and his navigator, Jean-Yves Bernot (who was off the boat for this leg), had spent the day before the race flying over the racecourse in a small plane. On start day Bernot was up in the air talking through strategy right up until the start. According to Frostad this exercise worked and the winning result proved it.

The biggest reception was for local favorite *illbruck*, who came in second. Kostecki and crew looked

djuice skipper Knut Frostad salutes in victory as he helms the boat into Kiel first to win leg nine.

extremely relieved to finish and win the overall prize. "What an awesome moment, it's just amazing," Kostecki said, smiling with the overall race trophy in his hands. "It's been hard work and intense racing for the past 9 months, and this moment makes it all worthwhile. We had an incredible battle on our hands as we had great competition from the other teams and they pushed us to fight for every point."

Finishing third for the leg and second overall, the hometown team of *Assa Abloy* became national heroes. The mastermind behind the campaign, Magnus Olsson, could not have been happier. *Assa Abloy* turned around two bad early legs to earn a lot of

Thousands of spectator boats surround illbruck *as she heads for the line in second place for leg nine to win the race.*

Leg Nine Results

Position	Yacht	Elapsed Time	Leg Points	Overall Points	Overall Standings
1	djuice	1 day 3 hours 42 minutes	8	33	6
2	illbruck	1 day 4 hours 17 minutes	7	61	1
3	Assa Abloy	1 day 6 hours 13 minutes	6	55	2
4	Amer Sports Too	1 day 6 hours 18 minutes	5	16	8
5	Amer Sports One	1 day 6 hours 19 minutes	4	44	3
6	SEB	1 day 8 hours 1 minute	3	32	7
7	Tyco	1 day 9 hours 27 minutes	2	42	4
8	News Corp	1 day 10 hours 11 minutes	1	41	5

Leg nine winner, djuice.

respect. "Our boat is beautiful. It's the best boat in the fleet and we've worked hard at it," said Neal McDonald. Mark Rudiger added, "I think we all have mixed feelings about the end. We're all ready for clo-sure, and to stop moving from boat to hotel to boat, etcetera. But we'll also miss the race, the singular focus, the awesome sailing, and the achievement."

The women on *Amer Sports Too* did it. They fin-ished fourth. They too were well received and were particularly happy to beat Dalton across the line. When Dalton arrived at the dock, they presented him with a pineapple. True to his word, Dalton stripped down to his shorts and stuffed the pineapple down the back. The crowd loved it! It was a good-natured moment.

SEB was next to cross. The decision to pass west of the island of Anholt had sealed her fate. With *djuice* winning the leg *SEB* ended up seventh overall. *Tyco* came into Kiel seventh.

Amer Sports Too, Day Two

Absolutely fantastic, we are really, really happy. It was a nice way to finish for the team because we always knew we had it in us. We've worked really hard and I think that has started to pay off for us. It's just a pity we haven't got a few more legs.

Lisa McDonald

It was well after midnight when *News Corp* fin-ished. Jez Fanstone and crew fell short with the west-ern course decision. "It's been torture. After 32,000 miles of ocean racing, it comes down to a buoy-filled lottery to a certain extent."

It truly was a fighting finish for every boat. There was elation and disappointment. Jez Fanstone summed up the experience brilliantly. "If you dare to dream, you're bound to have a few nightmares along the way."

The women on Amer Sports Too *lead the men on* Amer Sports One *into Kiel by a fraction of a mile.*

Knut Frostad's team djuice *receives its Waterford crystal trophy for first place in leg nine and for sixth position overall.*

Race One: 1973–1974

Race Two: 1977–1978

Race Three: 1981–1982

Race Four: 1985–1986

Race Five: 1989–1990

Race Six: 1993–1994

Race Seven: 1997–1998

Part Four
Round the World
History

Like climbing Mount Everest or trekking to the North Pole, the idea of circumnavigating the globe in a sailing boat stirs the imagination of sailors and non-sailors alike. From our earliest days in school, the courageous explorers who went searching the world were the heroes of our textbooks. Marco Polo, Leif Ericson, Vasco da Gama, Ferdinand Magellan, Sir Francis Drake, and Christopher Columbus have historically been portrayed as larger than life. But imagine the ridicule these explorers received as they sailed over the horizon in those early days of discovery. Most people believed the world was flat, but the incentive of treasure, trade, new territory, curiosity, and glory drove those undaunted adventurers from safe harbors to the distant unknown.

As explorers grew more ambitious and their adventures more extensive, they required more from their vessels. Ships had to be faster, able to hold more cargo, and carry growing rosters of sailors, scientists, and soldiers.

Early heavy wooden ships had difficulty sailing upwind, but the hulls and rigs became more efficient as design technology advanced, based on sailors' experience navigating the wind and waves of the open oceans. Christopher Columbus, for example, had a secret that he kept to himself. He knew that at latitude 10 degrees north the prevailing wind was out of the east, while at 40 degrees north the wind blew out of the west. Columbus was able to sail downwind to the New World on the southern route and downwind again on his return by first heading north.

Over the centuries, mariners learned that there were helpful prevailing winds all around the globe. As this knowledge was gained and passed on, global commerce grew. The clipper ships used the advantageous winds to deliver precious cargo.

There's no doubt that early sailing masters pushed their vessels and crew hard to be the first into port, foretelling an era when ships would be used for sport.

Designer Donald McKay became a legend in the 1850s for his fast, reliable clipper ships. According to Felix Reisenberg in his book *Cape Horn* (Dodd, Meade and Company, 1939), between 1850 and 1874, 22 clipper ships sailed from New York to San Francisco in fewer than 100 days. These ships averaged 5.3 knots. In 1851, the yacht *America* sailed around the Isle of Wight at an average speed of 5.1 knots to claim the 100 Guinea Cup, sport's oldest trophy, later renamed the America's Cup. Spurred on by *America's* victory and the rising popularity of yacht racing, McKay started building ships like *Great Republic* in 1853 specifically to break records. The reward of prize money helped the sport grow even more.

It was the spirit of these historic, competitive clipper ships that inspired the first round-the-world race in 1973, organized by the Royal Naval Sailing Association and sponsored by the Whitbread Beer Company. A few years before, solo-circumnavigators like Sir Francis Chichester and Robin Knox-Johnston had earned worldwide acclaim for their successful passages around the planet. The Whitbread Round The World Race visionaries were mindful of the respect Chichester and Knox-Johnston received after their triumphant feats.

The first Whitbread Round The World Race attracted adventurers, military men, and even a few professional yacht racers. Simply finishing the contest was considered an amazing accomplishment. Over the course of 3 decades, The Whitbread evolved into an increasingly competitive race, and just as Donald McKay crafted his speedy ships 120 years ago, boats are now designed and built specifically for racing around the world.

Computer design programs, weather prediction modeling, wind tunnels, towing tanks, and strong, light-weight materials combine to give the Volvo Ocean 60s impressive speed. Today's V.O.60s sail at twice the speed of the clipper ships, just as the modern America's Cup Class yachts sail at twice the average speed of the schooner *America.*

The evolution of the Volvo Ocean Race has been a fascinating tale of sailors, designers, race officials, promoters, and media people, all helping to inspire the V.O.60s to sail faster on their quest to be first around the world.

Unlike the early sailors, whose stories were told months and years after their voyages, we now have instant access through the Internet to the drama, thoughts, emotions, images, positions, and weather experienced by the fleet as the boats race to their next port. Sea stories always captivate the listener or reader, so it is no accident historians give these explorers such prominent roles. Mariners have a way of turning romance into reality.

Race One
1973–1974

At sea—resolution. Ashore—goodwill.
In defeat—defiance. In victory—magnanimity.
Winston Churchill

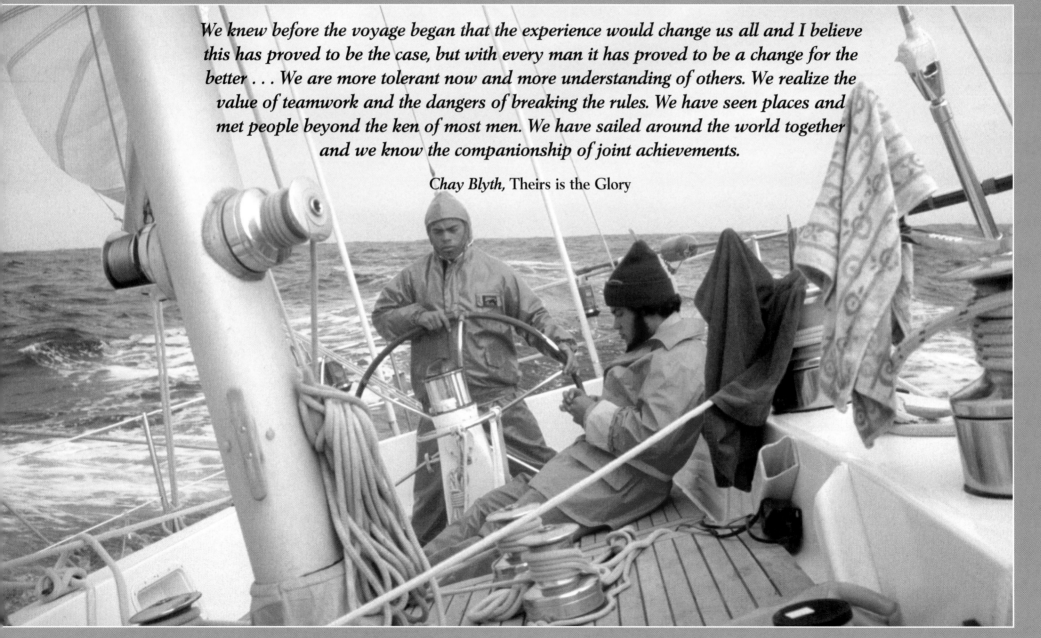

We knew before the voyage began that the experience would change us all and I believe this has proved to be the case, but with every man it has proved to be a change for the better . . . We are more tolerant now and more understanding of others. We realize the value of teamwork and the dangers of breaking the rules. We have seen places and met people beyond the ken of most men. We have sailed around the world together and we know the companionship of joint achievements.

Chay Blyth, Theirs is the Glory

Onboard Sayula II, 1973. Today, you would not see a crew sitting inboard or the towels out drying.

1973–1974

More like an extended adventure or an expedition along the lines of climbing Everest than a fierce yachting competition, the very first Whitbread Round The World Race attracted a variety of entries eager to test their sailing skills by facing the challenges and dangers of this new race.

The Whitbread Race began on a lovely morning in September 1973, amidst a crush of well-wishing spectator boats in the Solent, off Portsmouth, England. Many of the spectator boats could have been mistaken for the 17 yachts at the starting line; such was the nature of ocean racing yachts at that time. Two of the yachts had been built before World War II (Poland's *Otago* and Germany's *Peter von Danzig*), two had been built especially for the race (France's *Pen Duick VI* and *Kriter*), and two more had been refitted from the 1968 single-handed transatlantic race (UK's *Second Life* and France's *33 Export*). The British Navy's entry, *Adventure*, was to change crews at each of the four stops on her way around the world, and many other boats would substitute crewmembers as well, so that while 163 were on board the yachts at the start, there would be 324 who ultimately competed in at least part of this inaugural race. Despite the notoriously short preparation time, almost all crews ate well, and some yachts even carried a few cases of good wine.

A crucial element in the accomplishment of this first-ever round-the-world yacht race was the Royal Naval Sailing Association. Their seafaring experience, knowledge, and global contacts, as well as the use of the British Navy's principal port near Portsmouth, England, provided necessary race support from weeks before the start right through to the finishing gun, seven months later. This was a heavily service-propelled event: The British Army also entered a 59-foot ketch, *British Soldier*, and Chay Blyth, aboard *Great Britain II*, was accompanied by fellow members of his Parachute Regiment.

The first leg of this 27,000-mile sailing race to Cape Town, South Africa, was marked by a squall that took *Great Britain II*'s crewman Bernie Hosking over the side, but his crewmates searched for and found him by flashlight beam after the light on the life buoy failed.

Almost immediately after the start of the second leg, Cape Town to Sydney, Australia, most of the fleet felt the brunt of strong southeast winds. *Burton Cutter* began to break up, but ingenious repairs made by skipper Leslie Williams got the boat safely to Port Elizabeth, South Africa. Aboard *Burton Cutter* was a young New Zealander named Peter Blake, getting a taste for the race in which he would ultimately star.

In a fierce southwesterly, *Tauranga* suffered a broach and spar breakage. During efforts to prevent further damage, crew member and British soldier Paul Waterhouse was flung to the deck, then knocked overboard, probably unconscious. The crew searched

Day 14 out of Cape Town, John Rist's log

We are sustaining so much damage in these seas that it is a wonder there is a bloody boat left.

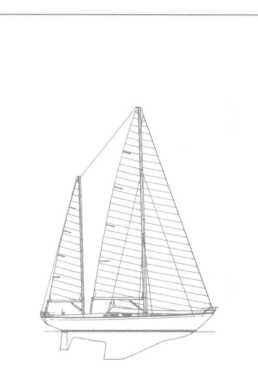

Profile of Sayula II—*Winner of the 1973–74 Whitbread Round The World Race.*

Skipper—Ramon Carlin, Mexico
Designer—Sparkman & Stephens, USA
Builder—Nautor Swan, Finland
LOA—65 feet/19.8 meters
Beam—16.3 feet/5.0 meters
Displacement—56,370 pounds/25,590 kilograms

the surrounding waters for hours, but to no avail.

Just a week later, during an effort to further shorten sail on *33 Export* in severe gale conditions, a huge breaker swept Dominique Guillet overboard. After a futile 30-minute search, with worsening weather, the yacht was forced to run off. Understandably shaken, the crew sailed straight for Fremantle.

With the loss of two men, the advisability—much less sanity—of racing in such conditions was questioned, but the race continued, with all safety issues to be given extremely serious consideration at the end of the race.

The light air that plagued the race at the start of leg three was followed by a "Southerly Buster" in

1973–1974 Results

Position	Yacht	Nationality	Skipper(s)	* Corrected Time
1	Sayula II	Mexico	Ramon Carlin	133 days 13 hours
2	Adventure	United Kingdom	Patrick Bryans	135 days 8 hours
			Malcom Skene, George Vallings	
			Roy Mullender	
3	Grand Louis	France	André Viant	138 days 15 hours
4	Kriter	France	Jack Grout	141 days 2 hours
			Michel Malinovsky, Alain Gliksman	
5	Guia	Italy	Giorgio Falck	142 days 19 hours
6	Great Britain II	United Kingdom	Chay Blyth	144 days 11 hours
7	Second Life	United Kingdom	Roddy Ainslie	150 days 8 hours
8	CSeRB	Italy	Doi Malingri	155 days 7 hours
9	British Soldier	United Kingdom	James Myatt	156 days 21 hours
10	Tauranga	Italy	Eric Pascoli	156 days 22 hours
11	Copernicus	Poland	Zygfryd Perlicki	166 days 19 hours
12	33 Export	France	Jean-Pierre Millet	175 days 22 hours
			Dominique Guillet	
13	Otago	Poland	Zdzislaw Pienkawa	178 days 9 hours
14	Peter von Danzig	Germany	Reinhard Laucht	179 days 15 hours
DNF	Pen Duick VI	France	Eric Tabarly	—
DNF	Burton Cutter	United Kingdom	Leslie Williams, Alan Smith	—
DNF	Jakaranda	South Africa	John Goodwin	—
DNF	Concorde	France	Pierre Chassin	—
DNF	Pen Duick III	France	M. Cuiklinski	—

*Corrected time takes the handicap into account

Winner of the 1973–74 Whitbread Round The World Race, Ramon Carlin, Skipper of Sayula II.

the Tasman Sea, an intense frontal system with violent wind changes. *Great Britain II* lost main and mizzen spinnakers, *Sayula II* had to run off but even so damaged headsails. Then Chay Blyth decided to put up more sail, and in the process, Bernie Hosking lost his balance and fell overboard—for the second time this race. Despite a 2-hour search, this time Bernie was not found, resulting in the third tragic fatality of the race.

As the race continued toward Cape Horn, the yachts chanced 500-foot icebergs and their "calves" in the 50 and 60 south latitudes to take advantage of the easterlies. None had radar aboard in 1974. To shorten the distance and sail more northerly, the yachts were buffeted by contrary winds. Even *Adventure*, sailing close to 60 degrees south for 12 days, had winds ahead of her beam for the most part. This northerly versus southerly route to the Horn was to be debated over the course of future Whitbread races.

Great Britain II was the first to round Cape Horn, 26 days out from Sydney. Skipper Chay Blyth was one of the few Whitbread sailors to have sailed those waters before. Rounding the Horn was exciting for all sailors, especially those aboard *Adventure*; they were saluted enthusiastically by the British Naval guard ship as they rounded, with a salvo of blanks, of course . . . except that the wadding from one round tore through *Adventure's* headsail.

Constantly there was the deafening banging and flapping of sheets and sails as they were crucified by the 40-knot wind. The continuous hiss of the spray and the intermittent crashing of the waves onto the yacht made mad background music for the chaos being wreaked.

Chay Blyth, Theirs is the Glory

Pen Duick VI *crashing through the waves during the first Whitbread Round The World Race.*

Notes from the log

Life on board

Day 17 out of England, John Rist's log:
We had a very good breakfast, cornflakes, fruit juice, fried egg and freshly baked bread . . . we had spaghetti bolognese for dinner, which made a change.

14 Days out of Cape Town:
Before we left, the experts said the Roaring Forties would test the yacht and its crew. They were absolutely right. At the moment the deck looks like a scrap metal yard.

Eddie, with his one good hand, is proving a master chef. Tonight he prepared stewed steak, fish pie, and cake.

15 days out of Cape Town:
Late tonight I decided to match Eddie's culinary achievements by cooking crêpes Suzette for everyone . . . I used three-quarters of a bottle of brandy and as a result the crêpes tasted beautiful. I had two myself and felt quite giddy.

New Year's Eve 1973 celebration:
. . . We toasted the New Year with a drink from Alan's Ne'er Day Bottle and ate a piece of black bun . . . We wished each other a good New Year and drank to absent friends, had a good yarn and retold a few jokes. . . tiredness and thoughts of our families sent us all to bed—except of course the Watch.

On crew considerations:
I had private reasons for wanting a girl to be considered [Sue Manderson as cook]. There is no doubt that a female on board provides a stablizing factor. Men are better behaved, better dressed, and there is less swearing. They are also more careful about their habits and their attitudes.

Day 4 out of Sydney:
A heavy rain squall blew up . . . so I ordered everyone below to have a cup of tea and wait for the dawn. Only the helmsman stayed on deck and he was busy because even with just the rags of the spinnaker we were being blown along at about 5 knots and when we picked up a wave, we shot forward at 7 knots.

Heading for Cape Horn

Blows of up to 45 knots were commonplace and the legions of waves were towering over 40 feet. With the reacher up we made around 12 to 14 knots but when we hit a wave right and surfed on its crest we could manage well over 20 knots.

This was sailing at its most exhilarating and its most dangerous . . . We can now take stock of the damage caused by this constant beating: Three bulkheads are cracked, plus one bearer. Two shelves have been ripped away. One sheet has been chafed through. We have a very bad leak.

Sunday, January 6th, 1974, is a day that will live in my mind forever . . . it started casually enough, quite a clear morning with the wind Force 5 gusting to Force 6 . . . Suddenly our world was shattered as John Rist shouted that dreaded phrase: "Man overboard!" In such conditions it was almost unbelievable . . . "Luff up!" I cried . . . At the same time, I looked aft to glimpse a blue bundle being left astern in our wake. It was Bernie Hosking.

A life buoy was thrown after him immediately . . . we were trying to beat back all the time and the reacher sheet snapped, so down came the reacher. By now it was gusting Force 7 from the west and the men were working grimly and quickly . . . Apart from essential orders no one said a word. The minutes ticked away and although on two occasions we caught sight of the empty dan buoy there was no sign of Bernie . . .

After two hours I began to accept the dreadful fact that Bernie was dead . . .

We decided to press on to Rio. Death is a very personal thing and so final that there is little point in discussing it . . . I knew that Bernie would rarely be mentioned between us on the rest of the voyage and that such silence was a mark of respect for him.

Chay Blyth and his crewmate, John Rist, from Theirs is the Glory.

Sayula II, *winning entry in the first Whitbread Round The World Race.*

Crew of Second Life *from the United Kingdom.*

Rio de Janeiro's world-famous Carnival coincided with the round-the-world racers' layover in that city, and all the crewmembers were ready to whoop it up after the two most difficult legs of their race.

The fourth and final leg, from Rio de Janeiro back to Portsmouth, was the shortest leg, but with the most varied weather conditions to consider. The race committee had decided on a pursuit race, with the smaller boats starting first, so that small and large boats would finish together for a spectator fiesta. This was the Whitbread's single attempt at maximizing publicity through manipulation of the start.

The fleet took differing tactics crossing the Atlantic, ultimately bringing a sinking *Great Britain II* into Plymouth for line honors on April 9th, 1974. She had been 144 days at sea, setting a record for a round-the-world passage under sail.

Sayula II, a Sparkman & Stephens–designed ketch, won the first Whitbread Round The World Race on corrected time. Mexican owner Ramon Carlin accepted the Whitbread Trophy from the Admiral of the Royal Naval Sailing Association, His Royal Highness Prince Philip. At the ceremony, the organizers announced that the race would be held again, starting 4 years after the first race, in 1977.

Race Course for the first Whitbread Round The World Race 1973–1974

Leg 1—Portsmouth to Cape Town

Leg 2—Cape Town to Sydney

Leg 3—Sydney to Rio de Janeiro

Leg 4—Rio de Janeiro to Portsmouth

27,000 miles

Leg 1—Portsmouth to Cape Town
The first leg, of 6,650 nautical miles, began on September 8, 1973.

Leg 2—Cape Town to Sydney
The 6,550-nautical-mile leg began on November 7, 1973.

Leg 3—Sydney to Rio de Janeiro
The longest and arguably the most dangerous leg of the race, covering 8,370 nautical miles. The fleet left Sydney on December 29, 1973.

Leg 4—Rio de Janeiro to Portsmouth
The last leg was run as a pursuit race to reduce lag time between the first and the last boat into port. The boats set sail between March 6 and 11, 1974, on the final leg of 5,430 nautical miles.

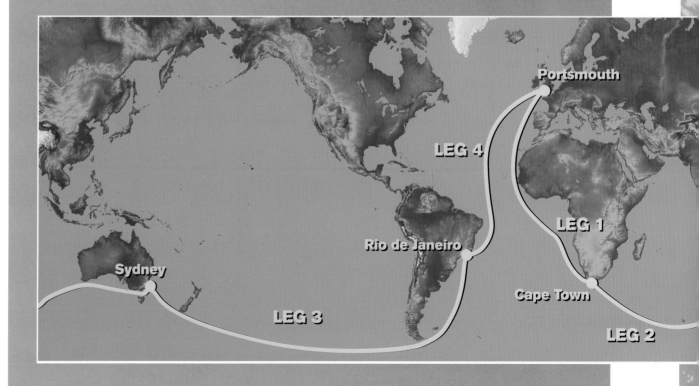

Race Two
1977–1978

It was not really about racing back then, although we did race hard. Adventure and seeing the world was the real attraction.

Skip Novak

Peter Blake at home on the wheel in the Southern Ocean.

1977–1978

The success of the first race brought more entries looking for the glamour of the experience, although sailing around the world competitively with just four stops lured more famous racing sailors than before. Some boats were designed especially for this race, and there was growing international interest.

On August 27, 1977, 15 yachts from six countries lined up to participate in what had become a classic race. The inaugural race had posed questions about safety and rules that had been addressed in the intervening 4 years. The minimum size had been increased to 55 feet. The maximum size (70 foot rating) was dictated by the IOR "maxi" rule. The winner would be the boat with the best aggregate corrected time over all legs, large or small. The race remained monohulls-only, because multihulls were unable to comply with requirements for crew and space for food and supplies.

Safety regulations included the compulsory fitting of jackstays in hopes of preventing future deaths. By clipping their safety harnesses to the jackstay, crew members would be far less likely to be separated from the boat if swept overboard.

Three of the boats had competed in the previous race: *Great Britain II*; *33 Export*, re-rigged to

The tall rig on Heath's Condor *helps the boat use wind aloft to sail in virtually no wind.*

a fractional sloop, and with the youngest skipper, 23-year-old Alain Gabbay; and *Adventure*, once again entered as a Ministry of Defence training yacht, and causing controversy with large crew changes.

Great Britain II was skippered by Rob James, who had crewed on *Second Life* in the last race and was an associate of *GBII's* previous skipper, Chay Blyth, in a charter firm. As in the first race, *Great Britain II's* 18-man crew paid for their places aboard: £4000 each.

Cornelis van Reitschoten, who came to be known as the "Flying Dutchman," was making his Whitbread debut on *Flyer*, a Sparkman & Stephens–designed 65-foot ketch. Typically, Rod Stephens was working aboard before the start. His firm's yachts would take the first five places in this race.

Clare Francis was the first woman skipper, aboard *ADC Accutrac*. Her new husband, Jacques, a Frenchman who had previously sailed aboard *Burton Cutter*, was among the crew of 12, as were two other women.

Skip Novak made his Whitbread debut as navigator aboard *King's Legend*, the third Swan 65 entered, *Disque d'Or* and *ADC Accutrac* being the others.

The race began in a light northerly that built dramatically, blowing out two of Francis's spinnakers, and one on *Heath's*

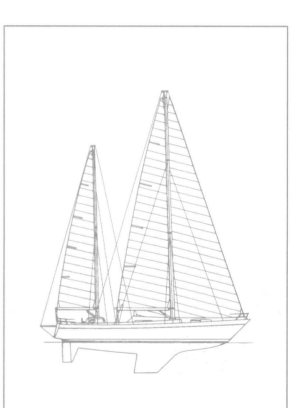

Profile of Flyer—*Winner of the 1977–78 Whitbread Round The World Race.*

Skipper—Cornelis van Rietschoten, Netherlands
Designer—Sparkman & Stephens, USA
Builder—Huisman-Vollenhove, Netherlands
LOA—65.1 feet/19.8 meters
Beam—16.3 feet/5.0 meters
Displacement—55,000 pounds/25,000 kilograms

. . .(France's 33 Export *was) directly behind* King's Legend, *and closing fast.* 33 Export *in fact over took them, then broached across* Legend's *bow; a horrible moment, just east of Cape Horn. A collision was narrowly avoided thanks to a little luck and very good helmsmanship.*

Aboard King's Legend, *a crew member prepares for a reef on the end of the boom. He holds on using his feet.*

Robin Knox-Johnston at the helm of Heath's Condor.

Condor (with veteran sailors Robin Knox-Johnson and Leslie Williams sharing the helm, and Peter Blake aboard).

Once again, the centuries-old round-the-world sailing routes were adjusted by the ability of the Whitbread boats to handle all sorts of weather and wind angles, unlike traditional square-riggers. But as in the first Whitbread, this did not preclude damage to boats and crew. They were racing, after all.

Heath's Condor was hit by a "nasty, squally day," according to Peter Blake, causing the mast to break and the boat to limp jury-rigged into the Liberian port of Monrovia.

With just 220 miles to Cape Town, *Flyer* was only 10 miles ahead of *King's Legend.* The two boats battled it out in varying wind conditions, with *Flyer* finishing just 2 hours ahead.

Sydney had been too confusing a port in the last

1977–1978 Results

Position	Yacht	Nationality	Skipper(s)	* Corrected Time
1	Flyer	Netherlands	Cornelis van Rietschoten	119 days 1 hour
2	King's Legend	United Kingdom	Nick Ratcliffe, Mike Clancy	121 days 11 hours
3	Traité de Rome	EEC	Philippe Hanin	121 days 18 hours
4	Disque d'Or	Switzerland	Pierre Fehlmann	122 days 10 hours
5	ADC Accutrac	United Kingdom	Clare Francis	126 days 20 hours
6	Gauloises II	France	Eric Loizeau	127 days 7 hours
7	Adventure	United Kingdom	James Watts, David Leslie Ian Bailey-Willmot Robin Duchesne	128 days 2 hours
8	Neptune	France	Bernard Deguy	130 days 11 hours
9	B&B Italia	Italy	Corrado di Majo	132 days 2 hours
10	33 Export	France	Alain Gabbay (31 min)	133 days 00 hours
11	Tielsa	Netherlands	Dirk Nauta (36 min)	133 days 00 hours
12	Great Britain II	United Kingdom	Rob James	134 days 10 hours
13	Debenhams	United Kingdom	John Ridgway	135 days 19 hours
14	Japy-Hermes	France	Jean Michel Viant	143 days 6 hours
15	Heath's Condor	United Kingdom	Leslie Williams Robin Knox-Johnston	144 days 00 hours

*Corrected time takes the handicap into account

race, so the fleet would sail on to Auckland, New Zealand. They had all that Southern Ocean to face, with the theoretical shortest course taking them directly over Antarctica. John Ridgway, aboard *Debenhams*, took the most southerly course, and eventually sailed straight into a field of ice, in a Force 9 gale, complete with snow. It took several hours, and full attention from all hands on deck to make way out of the pack ice and bergs and chunks, but they managed.

Speeds were startling for those days: *Heath's Condor* had a days' run of 267 miles, averaging 11.1 knots, with some moments beyond the 30-knot capabilities of the speedometer. Even the new safety rules initiated for this

race could not obviate accidents on this long and violent leg. When *Heath's Condor* lost Bill Abram over the side, Peter Blake crash-jibed the boat, the engine failed, and they lost sight of Abram. But a long 10 minutes later, Abram was rescued from the water, his position luckily given away by a circling flock of albatross. So much for the "Rhyme of the Ancient Mariner" . . . but still Peter Blake had to dive into the icy water and cut away a rope tangled in the prop.

Flyer made a best day's run of 281 miles, as the well-prepared yacht carried maximum sail not far behind the two maxis approaching Tasmania.

Auckland had the most enthusiastic welcome awaiting any of the Whitbread finishes.

Cornelis van Rietschoten—skipper of the Dutch yacht Flyer. *He demonstrated that good organization was the key to success.*

On November 25th, a huge crowd ashore and afloat cheered as *Heath's Condor* finished just over 30 days out from Cape Town. Fourteen days would separate her arrival from that of the struggling *Gauloises II*.

The topic of handicapping, which seemed to favor the smaller boats, was addressed, although not to the satisfaction of all. And there were some unique rating problems stemming from *Pen Duick VI's* spent-uranium keel (which eventually disqualified them) and *Heath's Condor's* carbon-fibre mast.

Very differently provisioned and outfitted compared with the spartan conditions on today's Volvo Ocean Race contestants, the cooks aboard the 1977–78 yachts were able to produce "parties" for New Year's celebrations, even under triple reef conditions, as aboard *Heath's Condor* off Chatham Island.

The long leg to Rio de Janeiro was officially won on January 28 when *Great Britain II* finished a scant 30 minutes ahead of *Heath's Condor*—half an hour's difference in a 32-day ocean race! The disqualified

After I retired I wanted to do something out of the ordinary.

Cornelis (Connie) van Reitschoten

The Dutch yacht Flyer *in the Solent after winning the 1977–78 Whitbread Round The World Race.*

Racing around the world in 1977 was adventure in a fairly true form. There were no back ups. I remember soon after we left New Zealand (having celebrated a double New Year's Eve while crossing the dateline!) we took a mild broach and the water in the aft head (yes we had two toilets on board!) emptied its contents into the SSB HF radio. Nobody seemed in the slightest annoyed nor worried about the fact we had no means of communicating with the shore or the other boats. Self sufficiency and self rescue was always understood. Navigation was with a sextant and a "time piece." As Dr. Johnson once said, conveniences are never missed where they were never enjoyed.

Skip Novak

On board Heath's Condor.

Pen Duick had finished several days before. Eric Taberly, a distinguished sailor, was however invited to continue to sail with the fleet "unofficially," and as such achieved second place on elapsed time, also "unofficially."

The 1977–78 Whitbread Round The World Race ended in foul weather and tatters: with squalls on March 23 as *Heath's Condor* blew out her spinnaker in full sight of the welcoming crowds at Portsmouth. *Flyer* finished in a full gale, with hail and 55-knot gusts. Within 5 days, all 15 boats had finished, with van Reitschoten having won on corrected time. This time there was no loss of life, and all boats were safely tucked in port.

. . . we had to use the barometer and

the clouds and the wind direction to

tell us what weather might be coming.

Satellite navigation hadn't come in . . .

We had to use the sextant . . .

Robin Knox-Johnston

The sextant was the most reliable way to navigate.

Race Course for the second Whitbread Round The World Race 1977–1978

Leg 1—Portsmouth to Cape Town

Leg 2—Cape Town to Auckland

Leg 3—Auckland to Rio de Janeiro

Leg 4—Rio de Janeiro to Portsmouth

26,780 miles

Leg 1—Portsmouth to Cape Town
The fleet left Portsmouth on August 27, 1977, for the first leg of 6,650 nautical miles.

Leg 2—Cape Town to Auckland
This 7,300-nautical-mile leg began from Cape Town on October 25, 1977.

Leg 3—Auckland to Rio de Janeiro
The third leg, covering 7,400 nautical miles, began on December 26, 1977.

Leg 4—Rio de Janeiro to Portsmouth
The final leg of 5,430 nautical miles started on February 22, 1978.

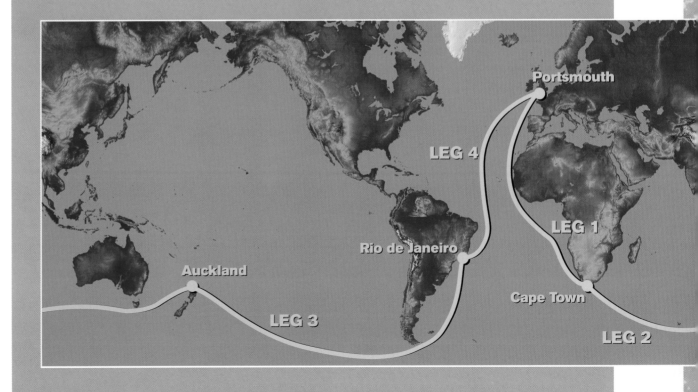

Race Three
1981–1982

The most boats from the most countries, the most designs, and the competition was set: serious racing sailors from around the world were eager to try once again to break records in this now-internationally acclaimed event.

With two jibs winged out and no mainsail, Flyer is stable speeding downwind in the Southern Ocean.

1981–1982

The third Whitbread Round The World Race began on August 29, 1981, when 28 boats representing 15 countries crossed the starting line off Portsmouth, England (a 29th entry, the Italian *Vivanapoli*, would start 5 days later). These competitors represented the most diverse fleet of boats ever to race around the world. The sheer number of competitors and support crews, as well as an influx of spectators, created a traffic problem both ashore and at sea around Portsmouth. Political problems undeniably existed between Great Britain and South Africa, yet Cape Town was the first port-of-call. At the last minute, the naval base was unavailable, and Camper and Nicholson's marina was substituted. This would be the last race started off Southsea Castle, because of both the retraction of British Naval support for a sporting event involving South Africa, and because crowd control was becoming unmanageable.

The variation in competing yachts was bracketed by two British entries, spanning the biggest at the 70-foot IOR maxi rule (*FCF Challenger* at 80 feet, LOA), all the way down to *Bubblegum*, at 43 feet, LOA. There was a little of everything in between, including Cornelis van Reitschoten's new *Flyer* and the old *Flyer*, now rechristened *Alaska Eagle*, and jointly skippered by Skip Novak and Neil Bergt.

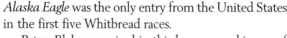

Alaska Eagle was the only entry from the United States in the first five Whitbread races.

Peter Blake was in his third race, as skipper of *Ceramco New Zealand*, and veterans Alain Gabbay (*Charles Heidsieck III*), Chay Blyth (*United Friendly*, ex-*Great Britain II*), Leslie Williams (*FCF Challenger*), Eric Taberly (*Euromarché*), and Pierre Fehlmann (*Disque d'Or*) also made return appearances.

The stopover in Rio de Janeiro was abandoned in favor of Mar del Plata, Argentina, where there was a branch of the Yacht Club Argentino. More than a thousand miles would be carved out of the third leg, and repetition of the excitement and over-stimulation of the last Whitbread stop in Rio de Janeiro, which resulted in police action, would be avoided.

Crew and boat preparations for the race had become more serious, intense, and much more safety-conscious. The boats were still relatively comfortable down below, although space-dividing bulkheads were disappearing with pipe berths more prevalent.

With so many boats competing, it was no surprise that the first leg of the race was marred by many incidents of gear failure and breakage. *Ceramco* was dismasted, but managed to limp into Cape Town in 18th place. Les Williams on *FCF Challenger*, again with paying crew aboard, lost time babying a splitting mast.

Checking the sails on board Flyer. *Chafe was a constant problem with the Dacron sails.*

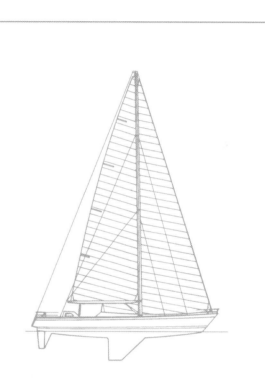

Profile of Flyer—*Winner of the 1981–82 Whitbread Round The World Race.*

Skipper—Cornelis van Rietschoten, Netherlands
Designer—German Frers, Argentina
Builder—Huisman-Vollenhove, Netherlands
LOA—76 feet/23.2 meters
Beam—18 feet/5.5 meters
Displacement—67,000 pounds/30,390 kilograms

Mending sails below deck.

1981–1982 Results				
Position	Yacht	Nationality	Skipper(s)	*Corrected Time
1	Flyer	Netherlands	Cornelis van Rietschoten	119 days 1 hour
2	Charles Heidsieck III	France	Alain Gabbay	120 days 7 hours
3	Kriter XI	France	Andre Viant	120 days 10 hours
4	Disque d'Or III	Switzerland	Pierre Fehlmann	123 days 11 hours
5	Outward Bound	New Zealand	Digby Taylor	124 days 11 hours
6	Xargo III	South Africa	Padda Kuttel	124 days 19 hours
7	Mor bihan	France	Phillipe Poupon	125 days 15 hours
8	Berge Viking	Norway	Peder Lunde	125 days 16 hours
9	Alaska Eagle	United States	Skip Novak, Neil Bergt	126 days 10 hours
10	Euromarche	France	Eric Tabarly	126 days 23 hours
11	Ceramco New Zealand	New Zealand	Peter Blake	127 days 17 hours
12	Skopbank of Finland	Finland	Kenneth Gahmberg	128 days 15 hours
13	RollyGo	Italy	Giorgio Falck	129 days 20 hours
14	Traité de Rome	EEC	Antonio Chioatto	130 days 23 hours
15	Croky	Belgium	Gustaaf Versluys	133 days 23 hours
16	FCF Challenger	United Kingdom	Leslie Williams	138 days 15 hours
17	United Friendly	United Kingdom	Blyth	141 days 10 hours
18	Walross III Berlin	Germany	Jean-Michel Viant	143 days 19 hours
19	Licor 43	Spain	Joaquin Coello	160 days 2 hours
20	Ilgagomma	Italy	Roberto Vianello	160 days 9 hours
DNF	European Uni. Belgium	Belgium	Jean Blondiau	—
DNF	33 Export	France	Phillipe Schaff	—
DNF	Gauloises III	France	Eric Loizeau	—
DNF	La Barca Laboratorio	Italy	Claudio Stampi	—
DNF	Save Venice	Italy	Doi Malingri	—
DNF	Vivanapoli	Italy	Beppe Panada	—
DNF	Scandanavian	Sweden	Reino Engqvist	—
DNF	Swedish Entry	Sweden	Mogens Bugge	—
DNF	Bubblegum	United Kingdom	Iain McGowan-Fyfe	—

*Corrected time takes the handicap into account

Of the 29 boats racing, 21 arrived at Cape Town reporting damage.

Cornelis van Reitschoten on *Flyer*, ahead the entire race, set a new course record, and beat the old *Flyer's* 1977 time by 2 days and 10 hours, as well as finishing 52 hours ahead of the second boat, *Charles Heidsieck III*. *Vivanapoli's* crew had been arrested and held as "spies" in Luanda, Angola, after the crew members' South African visas were found during a boarding by the crew of an Angolan gunboat, 150 miles at sea. *Vivanapoli* finally got to Cape Town 8 days after the start of the second leg.

With better-prepared boats and with the experience of two races, this second leg to Auckland was less terrifying, and certainly less lethal, than it had been in previous efforts. Even so, there were dismastings, many, many broken spars, and sails blown out, repaired, and blown out again. One crewman from *Outward Bound* was knocked overboard, but he was fished out of the cold sea quickly, thanks to having his harness clipped on.

Flyer finished first overall but Blake's *Ceramco New Zealand* finished second by a scant 12 hours, firing the New Zealanders' already high enthusiasm for the race. *Ceramco* had been able to take advantage of the famous tailwinds on this leg, managing to fly before 45 to 50-knot blasts. She claimed one 24-hour run of 316 miles, a record at the time, meaning an average sustained speed of 15 knots.

The round-the-Horn leg started with enthusiastic holiday crowds of New Zealanders thronging to the docks in Auckland, and more afloat to wish the boats bon voyage. Just 23 boats started what would prove to be an unusually mild and ice-free leg, with *Flyer* crossing the finish line first just 24 days after the start. *Charles Heidsieck* finished this leg fourth, but on corrected time was ahead of *Flyer* by 92 hours.

Discrepancies in finishing times, and the need for repairs due to gear breakage and failures, meant that the stopover in Mar del Plata lasted six weeks. This led race organizers to reconsider including such a wide range of competitors.

Everywhere else on the globe, there are land masses to check the sea's progress. But down south, between the Antarctic ice shelf and the southernmost capes of South Africa, Australia, New Zealand, and South America, the oceans roll unobstructed all the way around the world. Low pressure systems sweep through these ocean wastes with a frequency and velocity that has led to the various high lattitudes being dubbed the Roaring Forties, the Furious Fifties, and the Screaming Sixties.

Peter Blake

Above: The view from the end of the spinnaker pole shows a cluttered deck layout. Compare this shot with the layouts of the V.O.60s.

It is cold and lonely in the Southern Ocean.

Despite the huge expanses of water, even in the early days of the race, the racing could be incredibly tight. On day 30 out of Mar del Plata, the following radio conversation took place between Conny van Rietschoten aboard Flyer and Peter Blake aboard Ceramco New Zealand:

Conny: "Ceramco, this is Flyer. Peter, if I ever do this race again, I will do it differently."

PJB: "How, Conny?"

Conny: "In a much bigger and faster yacht. I'm tired of looking over my shoulder to find you biting at my heels."

Moving the jib leads was a continuous task.

A young Grant Dalton (second from right) takes the big wave in stride aboard Ceramco New Zealand.

The varying conditions for the transatlantic crossing required smart sailing in strong winds, and smarter sailing in lighter winds. Managing weather patterns was an enormous part of the passage. *Flyer*, and behind her, *Ceramco*, stayed in the wind, unlike *Charles Heidsieck*, which gave *Flyer* the time she needed for a first overall. After briefly running aground on the Shingles Bank, *Flyer* finished on March 29, 1982, the sure winner on elapsed time. *Ceramco* hit unfavourable winds in the Channel and finished three and a half days later. *Charles Heidsieck* and *Kriter IX* had suffered headwinds, and finished better than 105 hours after *Flyer*, giving *Flyer* the double win as well as a new Whitbread Race record.

Cornelis van Reitschoten and his *Flyer* program were much admired and copied. The intense preparation and the attention to all aspects of the boat's requirements during the stopovers had produced a boat that seemed to get better and stronger as the race progressed. The rest of the fleet finished with various breaks, leaks, and jury-rigs. *Vivanapoli* brought up the rear, finally finishing one month after *Flyer*.

A crew that is standing is an indication that the finish line is near as Ceramco New Zealand *arrives in Auckland.*

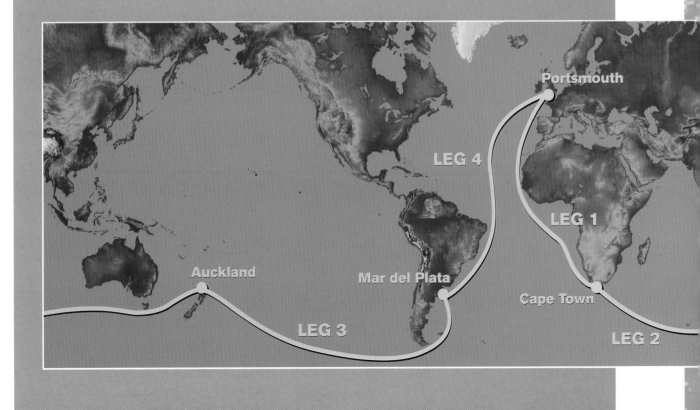

Race Course for the third Whitbread Round The World Race 1981–1982

Leg 1—Portsmouth to Cape Town

Leg 2—Cape Town to Auckland

Leg 3—Auckland to Mar del Plata

Leg 4—Mar del Plata to Portsmouth

26,095 miles

Leg 1—Portsmouth to Cape Town
The race began on August 8, 1981, with a first leg of 6,650 nautical miles.

Leg 2—Cape Town to Auckland
The 7,300-nautical-mile second leg began on September 30, 1981.

Leg 3—Auckland to Mar del Plata
The fleet set sail December 26, 1981 on the 6,175-nautical-mile third leg.

Leg 4—Mar del Plata to Portsmouth
The fourth and final leg—5,970 nautical miles—began on February 27, 1982.

Portsmouth

LEG 4

LEG 1

LEG 3

Auckland

Mar del Plata

Cape Town

LEG 2

Race Four
1985–1986

That's what the Whitbread Race is all about . . . sticking it out in bad times as well as in the good . . . and taking it one leg, one day, and then even one watch at a time.

Skip Novak, One Watch at a Time

Even with reduced sail Drum's leeward rail is awash. The crew is talking about reducing sail further.

1985–1986

To understand what it is like to repair, for example, a blown spinnaker at sea, think of approximately 4,700 square feet of sail, of a complicated panel design, ripped to shreds and immersed in sea water. Next imagine that sodden, tangled mass in a space the size of a small bathroom with a hair dryer, a pair of scissors, and a sewing machine. Finally, imagine trying to put it back together.

Skip Novak, One Watch at a Time

The smallest Whitbread Round The World Race winner has her day: little *L'Esprit d'Equipe* takes the race against even the mighty maxi class, and causes changes in the rating system as a result.

This fourth Whitbread Race consisted of mostly sponsored yachts, no military service entries, and no privately funded entries, with the possible exception of Simon Le Bon's *Drum*, and *SAS Baia Viking*, mostly private despite sponsored name. The Falklands War had broken out just after the last Whitbread's stopover in Mar del Plata, Argentina, so the South American stopover was changed once again, this time to Punta del Este, Uruguay. While there were questions about South Africa's suitability as a port of call, especially from New Zealand, it remained on the schedule for this race.

Most of the entries had paid attention to previous successful Whitbread contenders, and many were maxi-rated, but the winner turned out to be one of the smallest entries, carrying the fewest crew (eight): *L'Esprit d'Equipe* was actually the 1981–82 contender, *33 Export*.

On the wind, Atlantic Privateer.

At 58.5 feet, she was 23 feet shorter than the biggest entry, 83-foot *Côte d'Or*. *L'Esprit d'Equipe* was the last boat to win on corrected rather than elapsed time.

Changed port-of-call arrangements forced a later start than usual, and British Naval considerations once again took the start away from Portsmouth. Boats were berthed at Gosport, and the start took place off Spithead, with Dame Naomi James, widow of the late Rob James, firing the starting cannon on September 28, 1985.

As ever, there were last-minute changes amongst the fleet. The venerable *Great Britain II* was racing in its fourth Whitbread. Bob Salmon finalized sponsorship just the day before starting the boat as *Norsk Data GB*. More nations (10) were represented in this race proportionate to the number of starters (15) than in any other race.

Among the fleet was *Drum*, skippered by the veteran Skip Novak. *Drum* had weathered the vicious 1985 Fastnet race, but had spectacularly lost her keel and rolled over. The Whitbread's later start, combined with tremendous

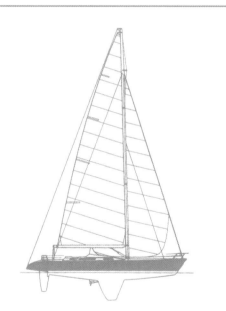

Profile of L'Esprit d'Equipe—*Winner of the 1985–86 Whitbread Round The World Race.*

Skipper—Lionel Péan, France
Designer—Phillipe Briand, France
Builder—Labb and Richeux/Dufour, France
LOA—57.7 feet/17.6 meters
Beam—15.8 feet/4.8 meters
Displacement—32,930 pounds/14,935 kilograms

Sailing Conditions

It was a cold morning, the air temperature was 3 degrees Celsius and I remember our watch was glad to get below looking forward to some decent sleep, secure in the knowledge that the right sail was up for the conditions. We were down below for no more than 10 minutes, shedding our foul weather gear in the forepeak and sipping mugs of coffee when *Drum* again became unstable and rolled violently to weather indicating the helmsman was steering too low. He made one recovery, but the die was cast, and as he rolled out for the second time we knew it was curtains. As we grappled to hand onto what ever was handy, while cursing him roundly, we waited for the inevitable crash, but *Drum* came quietly to rest on her side, pinned down by the spinnaker gently licking the surface of the water.

For the second time we had gybed her "Chinese" or "all standing" . . .

. . . it was as much a shambles below as it was on deck. Groggy heads popped out from behind the curtains in the bunk modules, scowling and swearing, only to be peppered by paperback books, cassette tapes, and other carelessly stowed items.

. . . The spinnaker was still full and drawing, holding us securely on our side. The sheet and lazy-guy winches were three feet under water and inaccessible. The cleated lazy-guy was taking the sheet load, and the trip line had jammed with the pole end submerged. In an act of courage, Mario went forward and eased off the halyard. In a shower of sparks, the wire raced through the winch drum and the tail shot out like cannon fire through the blocks and *Drum* slowly struggled to her feet . . .

. . . With the spinnaker still fluttering above the surface of the water and no major damage done, I had a feeling that we had got out of this too easily. No sooner had the thought left my mind than the over-size parachute lifted clear of the water as the boat got underway and promptly blew back into the after rigging taking out the weatherfax antenna, bending the Sat-Nav antenna and ripping off the after deck floodlight, before tearing itself to pieces on the backstays and again going overboard.

. . . The worst was yet to come.

The deck was a shambles of wires, ropes, and hardware in incredible tangles . . . Instinctively I went below and had a peek through our viewing tube directly above the propeller. My worst fears were justified when I spyed what I presumed to be the bright yellow, spinnaker turtle streaming from the now fully opened two-blade feathering propeller.

. . . I did not hesitate to call on Micky, our diver, to suit up and prepare the mini-dive bottle . . . The water temperature was just above the freezing point, but the biggest danger was the condition of the sea. We were in a full-blown gale in the Southern Ocean.

. . . The mistake we made was placing his [Micky's] lead block on the rail too far aft and playing out too much slack that allowed him to be shunted to the other side.

. . . as I looked aft, I could see him taking a terrible battering under the stern counter as the transom rose and fell 3 feet.

I can't remember, I think it was on the third or fourth toss that he [Micky] caught the line and with one big heave and a lucky wave, we landed him up on the transom like a big black fish . . . he was okay, but no one had to remind us that we had come close to losing a man.

Skip Novak, *One Watch at a Time*

For the brave crew member who climbs the mast there is a reward: it is quiet aloft.

A difference in round-the-world race styles was evident as future skipper Tracy Edwards was literally getting a taste for the Whitbread as cook aboard *Norsk Data*. She provided what were universally touted as excellent meals, a far cry from more recent weight-saving minimalist provisions.

December 4 was a month later than previous Cape Town starts, and weather conditions would prove to be different as well. The leg was marked by heavy-duty racing, as is inevitable in that part of the globe, with gear failures and breakage, men flung overboard but saved by their lifelines. *Atlantic Privateer*, having chosen an inshore finishing strategy, squeaked in ahead of *NZI Enterprise* by just half a mile, and 2 minutes. The other New Zealand entry, Peter Blake's *Lion*, finished after *UBS*, to a huge welcome.

An enormous spectator fleet saw the racers off in Auckland on February 15, 1986. But just 3 days out, *NZI* lost her mast in a Force 6 gale, and had to limp back to the Chatham Islands for what they hoped would be repairs. When that proved impossible, they had to withdraw from the race, a sad disappointment after their spectacular leg two finish.

effort, had allowed *Drum* to be ready for the gun.

More maxis than ever were racing this time, and to good advantage. Two-time competitor Pierre Fehlmann skippered *UBS Switzerland*, winning all legs but one, and the race overall on elapsed time.

Peter Blake, racing his fourth Whitbread aboard *Lion New Zealand*, had prepared thoroughly, and had worked closely with designer Ron Holland, a fellow New Zealander, to incorporate his on-the-water experience into the boat.

Eric Taberly, also making his fourth Whitbread attempt, had rushed through the construction of *Côte d'Or*, to finish just before the start. The longest yacht, but rating under maxi size, her best result was seventh on two legs, and 10th overall.

The September start was delayed because of weather. Radar was allowed aboard for the first time, which made the foggy Channel passage possible without incident. Daily position reports kept track of everyone, and the Doldrums were crossed without serious incident, although on widely different courses.

The leading five boats ran into severe southeasterly gales, fighting headwinds and a nasty cross-sea as they approached Cape Town. *Drum* and *Côte d'Or* suffered hull delamination from the pounding. *Atlantic Privateer* reported mast damage and put into Lüderitz, Namibia, for a temporary rig, which failed to get her the final 500 miles to Cape Town.

After 34 days, *UBS* crossed the finish line, followed by *Lion* 16 hours later, and just a tiny bit later by *Côte d'Or*.

Celebrating on board Drum *during the 1985–86 Whitbread.*

It cost each of the crew £8,000 to do the race on the boat [Norsk Data].
Karl and Chris, the two mates, and the only two who knew what they were doing, were on a different scheme. When I joined the boat, I was told all the crew had sailing experience, but it wasn't true. Then I discovered we were out of money. I was so busy provisioning and caught up in the whole affair that it wasn't until the morning of the start that I had second thoughts about going.

Tracy Edwards quoted by Skip Novak in *One Watch at a Time*

Lionel Péan, winning skipper of the 1985–86 Whitbread.

1985–1986 Results

Position	Yacht	Nationality	Skipper(s)	*Corrected Time
1	L'Esprit d'Equipe	France	Lionel Péan	111 days 23 hours
2	Philips Innovator	Netherlands	Dirk Nauta	112 days 21 hours
3	Fazer Finland	Finland	Michael Berner	115 days 00 hours
4	UBS Switzerland	Switzerland	Pierre Fehlmann	117 days 4 hours
5	Rucanor Tristar	Belgium	Gustaf Versluys, Ann Lippens	118 days 9 hours
6	Fortuna Lights	Spain	Javier Visiers, Jorgie Brufau Antonio Guiu	121 days 00 hours
7	Lion New Zealand	New Zealand	Peter Blake	121 days 7 hours
8	Drum	United Kingdom	Skip Novak	122 days 6 hours
9	Equity & Law	Netherlands	Pleun van der Lugt	123 days 6 hours
10	Cote d'Or	Belgium	Eric Tabarly	125 days 19 hours
11	Shadow of Switzerland	Switzerland	Otto & Nora Zehender-Mueller	128 days 11 hours
12	Norsk Data GB	United Kingdom	Bob Salmon	136 days 1 hour
13	SAS Baia Viking	Denmark	Jesper Norsk	144 days 18 hours
DNF	NZI Enterprise	New Zealand	Digby Taylor	—
DNF	Atlantic Privateer	United States	Padda Kuttel	—

*Corrected time takes the handicap into account

All boats headed well south for the shortest run to Punta del Este, with *Atlantic Privateer* taking a course 200 miles below the rest of the fleet and into the edge of the pack ice. Argos positioning put them ahead of *UBS* on this course. Nine days after the start, the Roaring Forties kicked in, and *UBS* set her heavy spinnaker, covering 303 miles in 24 hours, averaging 12.6 knots, with top speeds of 20 knots.

The weather in the Southern Ocean provides all the excitement a sailor can bear: long hours spent surfing down waves, and broaches not uncommon. *Drum* reported that an immense wave, almost vertical, had come up astern. The ride down ended when her nose dug into the trough, all the way to the main hatch. No breakage, no injuries, and *Drum* kept on racing.

Drum wasn't as lucky with a leeward broach that took out four stanchions, broke the spinnaker pole, and washed a spinnaker bag overboard to snug up against the prop. Crew member Magnus Olsson geared up and went into the freezing water to cut away the mess, but became trapped before he'd cleared it entirely. He was hauled aboard by his har-ness and safety line, but not before he had lost consciousness. He was taken below and revived, and the tangle cleared by a clever use of anchor-line rig.

Lion reported some spectacular iceberg sightings, and was averaging 260 to 280 miles a day. *L'Esprit's* mast suffered damage under hard running conditions, including a spinnaker broach and total knockdown. *Atlantic Privateer* also experienced a massive broach while surfing at high speed, causing cook Tracy Edwards' just-prepared meal to decorate the overhead rather than warm the crew's stomachs.

Rounding the Horn was fairly uneventful, too calm actually to suit the bigger boats in the lead, but some of the boats hit the pampero as they approached Punta del Este. First to finish in Punta del Este, *UBS* just got her sails down before 60-knot winds struck. Nine hours later, *Drum* finished 20 minutes ahead of *Atlantic Privateer*, who beat *Côte d'Or* by the same time. After 6,200 miles, for three boats to finish within an hour of each other was extraordinary.

A month later, on April 9, the fleet set out for Portsmouth, working its way up the Brazilian coast in fluky winds. The modern yacht designs did better through the Doldrums, and the smaller boats crept up on the bigger ones, banking their handicaps.

Early May provided choices as to how the fleet would handle the North Atlantic's springtime weather obstacle, the Azores High. Pierre Fehlmann, skipper of *UBS*, decided to chance the variable winds approaching western Europe, found a low that blew him home handsomely, and finished 2 days ahead of the fleet, winning the race on elapsed time. *Côte d'Or* was next in, followed just 4 hours later by *Drum*. But little *L'Espirit d'Equipe* won the Whitbread Round The World Trophy, presented by the late Diana, Princess of Wales; the last time the trophy would be awarded for corrected time.

L'Esprit d'Equipe *from France wins the 1985–86* Whitbread.

Race Course for the fourth Whitbread Round The World Race 1985–1986

Leg 1—Portsmouth to Cape Town

Leg 2—Cape Town to Auckland

Leg 3—Auckland to Punta del Este

Leg 4—Punta del Este to Portsmouth

26,740 miles

Leg 1—Portsmouth to Cape Town the fleet set sail from Portsmouth on September 28, 1985, for the 7,350-nautical-mile first leg.

Leg 2—Cape Town to Auckland The 7,300-nautical-mile second leg began on December 4, 1985.

Leg 3—Auckland to Punta del Este February 14, 1986, marked the start of the 6,215-nautical-mile third leg.

Leg 4—Punta del Este to Portsmouth The fourth and final leg of 5,875 nautical miles left Punta del Este on April 9, 1986.

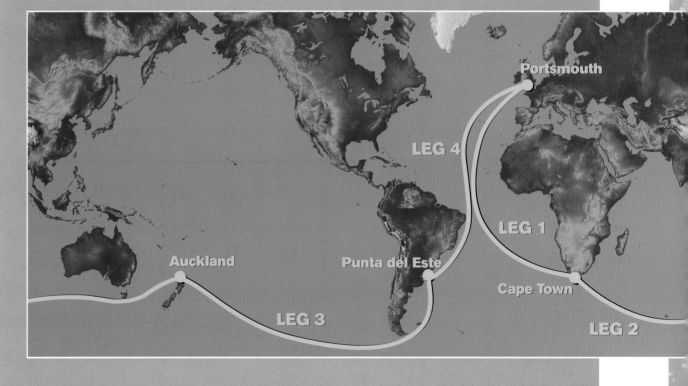

Race Five
1989–1990

"It took him five attempts to win at the Whitbread during which he experienced every set back from near sinking to dismasting before everything went right."

Cornelis van Rietschoten on Peter Blake's win on Steinlager 2

The fractional rig of the mighty red ketch Steinlager 2 proved to be a more efficient rig than the masthead configuration carried by Fisher & Paykel.

1989–1990

On 20 February we heard on the radio sched that Steinlager *and* Fisher & Paykel, *again not far away from each other, had rounded Cape Horn at 1130 GMT, almost 300 miles ahead of us. We had just been close reaching for the last 3 days, in miserable conditions, fighting to regain northing. It looked as if seven maxis would converge on Cape Horn within a few hours.*

Skip Novak, Fazisi

New Zealand puts its stamp on the race: winner Peter Blake bests Grant Dalton in a hotly contested match, and eight of the 23 starters are Farr Yacht Design boats.

Many changes marked this fifth Whitbread Round The World Race. They included providing trophies for each class rather than one overall winner on corrected time. The handicapping system itself was also changed, reducing the evident advantage given to the smaller boats in the past. By the end of the race, the IOR rating system, without which there arguably could never have been a first Whitbread Round The World Race, proved outdated except within the maxi class. Conflict between international yacht racing officials and the sponsors became quite heated, due to New Zealand's long-planned two-boat effort. *Steinlager 2* and *Fisher & Paykel*, both designed by Farr Yacht Design, had been built before some IOR rule changes were made that would have effec-

Maiden *during the 1989–90 Whitbread.*

tively excluded them from the race. This was resolved by reverting to the 1988 rules, as the boats had been built to them.

The fleet contained 17 maxis, and the second highest number of competitors to date. The British services were back in the race with *British Satquote Defender*, using crew from the army, navy, and air force. *Atlantic Privateer* was back as *Liverpool Enterprise*, and *Rothmans* had hot, small-boat sailor Lawrie Smith as skipper. The cruising class contained *Creightons Naturally* (ex-*FCF Challenger*) and *With Integrity* (ex-*Great Britain II*). Both had paying crews and limited sponsorship. The most newsworthy was the women's entry *Maiden*, Pierre Fehlmann's 1981 *Disque d'Or*, refitted and rebuilt for two-time Whitbread competitor, Tracy Edwards, and the first all-women crew. It was met with much skepticism and little sponsorship, to begin with, but the women finished their race on quite a different note.

Equally interesting was *Fazisi,*

Profile of Steinlager 2—*Winner of the 1989–90 Whitbread Round The World Race.*

Skipper—Peter Blake, New Zealand
Designer—Bruce Farr, New Zealand/USA
Builder—Southern Pacific, New Zealand
LOA—84 feet/25.6 meters
Beam—19.2 feet/5.85 meters
Displacement—68,000 pounds/30,845 kilograms

the first—and last—entry from the U.S.S.R. Whitbread veteran, Skip Novak, was contracted as co-skipper and took on the enormous task of preparing the boat and an inexperienced crew in just over 4 months.

Changes in the course were also made. Stopping in South Africa was definitely out for political reasons. This meant accommodating the long haul around the Cape of Good Hope with a stop in Punta del Este, Uruguay, before calling at Fremantle, Western Australia. Given New Zealand's fever and support for the race, a short hop would be made from Freo to Auckland. Then it would be back to Punta del Este, and since the United States was finally interested in this race, a stop in Ft. Lauderdale was planned before the transatlantic leg to the finish back in England. This increased the length of the race by some 5,000 miles, and the number of legs from four to six, which would cost more for competitors and take approximately 2 months longer to accomplish. The increase in media coverage and advertising exposure would presumably make it worthwhile.

The start from Southampton on September 2, 1989, sent the fleet off to South America rather than South

The Card during the first leg of the Whitbread 1989–90.

The best way to get up close during arrivals was by small, rubber craft.

Africa, and a brush with the Portuguese Trades brought northerly gales at 40 knots. *Steinlager 2* set a course record with an average speed of 14.3 knots, making 343 miles on a day's run. Good weather decisions—and their favorable conditions—put *Steinlager 2* more than 1,500 nautical miles ahead of the smaller boats as the latter hit the Doldrums close to the equator.

Race Committee estimates for the first leg were that it would take 30 days with winning speeds around 7.5 knots. In fact, it took *Steinlager 2* 25 days, 20 hours, and 46 minutes to finish first, and her average speed was 9.46 knots. The last boat in, Cruising Division's *With Integrity*, clocked 35 days.

The stay in Punta del Este was sadly marked by two non-sailing tragedies: the co-skipper of *Fazisi*, Alexei Grischenko, committed suicide, and *The Card's* crew member Janne Gustafson was killed in a motorcycle accident.

Despite the long stay in Punta del Este, the October 28 start for the next leg took place early enough in the Southern Hemisphere's summer for bad weather to be expected. Gale after gale tested all the boats as they made their way through the worst the Southern Ocean had to offer. Frightening broaches, even more so amidst icebergs; broken spars; rigging problems; and sail blowouts were all reported. Men did fall overboard (and a woman, too). All were either tethered to begin with or rescued safely. A broken arm and collarbone were handily taken care of, thanks to clever thinking and anticipatory preparations. *Fortuna*

Sailing under spinnaker with the wind at 30 knots
is fantastic but exhausting. Steering is exhilarating . . .
a slope of water as steep as a ski jump, glistening in
the moonlight like mercury, stretches downhill in front
of the boat. We plunge down the waves at amazing
speeds . . . Sheets of spray fly past, silver bullets of
water sting my face. This is what it's all about. This
is what makes all the risk and misery worthwhile.

Roger Vaughan, Day Seven out of Auckland
LIFE magazine, May 1990

On board Fazisi in the Southern Ocean.

Peter Blake hoists the trophy given to the winner of each leg. He would repeat this ritual after all six legs.

Extra Lights, a light displacement maxi, reported making over 400 miles in 24 hours (averaging 17 knots). Lawrie Smith, on *Rothmans*, reported an average speed of 19.9 knots over one 90-minute span.

On November 12, 1989, *Creightons Naturally* jibed in a westerly gale, broke a running backstay, then jibed again, tearing out two winch pedestals, and as the resulting mess was being attended to, two large seas swept Bart van den Dwey and Tony Phillips overboard. Both had on life jackets with flares and personal location devices. Both were rescued within the hour, and van den Dwey was quickly revived, but Phillips became the first

fatality since the first race in 1974.

That these two men were found as quickly as they were was thanks to the installation, by skipper John Crittenden, of VHF directional equipment exceeding race requirements. Aboard *Maiden*, Dr. Clare Russell shared essential advice about treating hypothermia and shock, which greatly aided the recovery of van den Dwey. *Maiden's* skipper, Tracy Edwards, also relayed messages during this crisis, and for this was given the British Telecom Communicator Award.

1989–1990 Results

Position	Yacht	Nationality	Skipper(s)	Elapsed Time
1	Steinlager 2	New Zealand	Peter Blake	128 days 9 hours
2	Fisher & Paykel NZ	New Zealand	Grant Dalton	129 days 21 hours
3	Merit	Switzerland	Pierre Fehlmann	130 days 10 hours
4	Rothmans	United Kingdom	Lawrie Smith	131 days 4 hours
5	The Card	Sweden	Roger Nilson	135 days 7 hours
6	Charles Jourdan	France	Alain Gabbay	136 days 15 hours
7	Fortuna Extra Lights	Spain	Javier de la Gaudera Jan Santana José Luis Doreste	137 days 8 hours
8	Gatorade	Italy	Giorgio Falck Hervé Jan Preire Sicouin	138 days 14 hours
9	Union Bank of Finland	Finland	Ludde Ingvall	138 days 16 hours
10	Belmont Finland II	Finland	Harry Harkimo	139 days 4 hours
11	Fazisi	USSR	Alexi Grischenko Skip Novak Valeri Alexeev	139 days 9 hours
12	NCB Ireland	Ireland	Joe English	139 days 19 hours
13	British Satquote Defender	United Kingdom	Frank Esson Colin Watkins	143 days 12 hours
14	Equity & Law II	Netherlands	Dirk Nauta	148 days 23 hours
15	Liverpool Enterprise	United Kingdom	Bob Salmon	151 days 4 hours
16	Creightons Naturally	United Kingdom	John Chittendon	162 days 6 hours
17	Esprit de Liberté	France	Patrick Tabarly	164 days 21 hours
18	Maiden	United Kingdom	Tracy Edwards	167 days 3 hours
19	Schlussel von Bremen	Germany	Rolf Renken Ham Müeller-Röhlok Jochen Orgelmann Wilhelm-Otto Beck Peter Weidner	167 days 19 hours
20	With Integrity	United Kingdom	Andy Coghill	170 days 16 hours
21	La Poste	France	Daniel Mallé	181 days 22 hours
DNF	Rucanor Sport	Belgium	Bruno Dubois	—
DNF	Martela OF	Finland	Markku Wilkeri	—

That Christmas means many different things to many different people could not be more true than on Fazisi . . . Eugene, in his blunt manner pointed out, It wasn't that long ago that anyone caught celebrating Christmas could be thrown in jail.

Skip Novak, Fazisi

On board Fazisi *during the 1989–90 Whitbread.*

The approach to Fremantle was exciting as the lead changed daily. After 27 days at sea, Peter Blake brought *Steinlager 2* into Fremantle an hour and a half ahead of the dueling *Rothmans* and *Merit*. Those two jibed 18 times in 20 minutes trying to establish an edge. Lawrie Smith's America's Cup experience finally put him ahead by just 28 seconds. *Fisher & Paykel* finished an hour and a half later. Tracy Edwards' *Maiden* finished first in her division a week later, having admirably struggled through filthy weather, and silencing the skeptics.

The short hop to Auckland provided rotten Tasman Sea weather, with broken spars, a dismasting, and a plague of whales, most of which were narrowly avoided or bumped without serious consequence. Christmas Day saw champagne and stocking presents being opened aboard *Maiden*. But it was freeze-dried food as usual aboard Peter Blake's *Steinlager 2*, as she battled it out with fellow New Zealander Grant Dalton on *Fisher & Paykel*. Both wanted to be first into home waters.

The leg finished in a New Zealand frenzy. After battling for the last 30 miles, *Steinlager 2* beat *Fisher & Paykel* by just 6 minutes. *Rothmans* and *Merit* repeated the excitement an hour later, finishing 10 minutes apart, after 3,272 miles at sea. *Maiden* again won the leg in her division.

After extravagant Auckland hospitality, the two New Zealand ketches had a screaming ride to Punta

The sloop Merit *could not keep up with the ketches* Steinlager 2 *and* Fisher & Paykel *even though she led at this moment.*

Tracy Edwards and her all-women's crew proved that they could be competitive at round-the-world racing by winning their class on leg two from Punta del Este to Fremantle.

del Este, in front of a 55-knot gale and in a nasty chop of a sea. This abated 10 miles out, with *Steinlager 2* finishing just 21 minutes ahead of *Fisher & Paykel*. *Rothmans* was less than an hour behind them.

The next leg, to Ft. Lauderdale, was a new course for the racers, through the very hot Tropics. Once again, *Steinlager 2*, *Fisher & Paykel*, and *Rothmans* all finished the leg within 5 hours of each other, putting on a fine show for the new United States port.

This layover lasted 30 days for the first in, and 22 days for *La Poste*, bringing up the rear, plenty of time for American sightseeing and various repairs, both major and minor, and even trips home. Feeling the thaw of the Cold War, the Russian crew aboard *Fazisi* was much fêted, to their bemusement.

During the layover, the first seeds were sown for the Whitbread 60 rule, in a conference for competitors, designers, yachting officials, journalists, and sponsors. The design concept was controversial, and many worried that a faster ride through the Southern Ocean might not be as safe a ride. But racing sailors now seemed interested in sailing as fast as possible, taking the safety considerations for granted, and being willing to eschew comfort altogether.

The start of the last leg was marred by unruly spectator fleet behavior, including a US Coast Guard cutter slicing across the racing fleet and causing emergency changes of course. But the boats were off and riding the Gulf Stream north along the coast. *Rothmans* had to put in to repair a broken shroud, ending her hopes of winning this leg, and several other boats suffered mast and rigging failures. The length of the race and the prolonged upwind work were causing inevitable wear and tear.

Sailing as far north as they did on the leg back to Southampton, the fleet was once again faced with ice warnings as they skirted the Labrador Current. Four days from the finish, the two New Zealand ketches were once again battling it out, but much to Grant Dalton's ongoing frustration, Peter Blake and his crew aboard *Steinlager 2* prevailed. On a fine day in May, they ghosted past the Needles at 10 knots under spinnaker to win the race, Blake's fifth and final Whitbread effort.

Steinlager 2 wins the 1989–1990 Whitbread.

Race course for the fifth Whitbread Round The World Race 1989–1990

Leg 1—Southampton to Punta del Este

Leg 2—Punta del Este to Fremantle

Leg 3—Fremantle to Auckland

Leg 4—Auckland to Punta del Este

Leg 5—Punta del Este to Fort Lauderdale

Leg 6—Fort Lauderdale to Southampton

32,018 miles

Leg 1—Southampton to Punta del Este
The fleet left Southampton on September 2, 1989, voyaging 5,938 nautical miles.

Leg 2—Punta del Este to Fremantle
This leg left Punta del Este for 7,260 nautical miles on October 28, 1989.

Leg 3—Fremantle to Auckland
This 3,272-nautical-mile leg began on December 23, 1989.

Leg 4—Auckland to Punta del Este
February 4, 1990, marked the start of this 6,255-nautical-mile leg.

Leg 5—Punta del Este to Fort Lauderdale
Leg five covered 5,475 nautical miles, beginning on March 17, 1990.

Leg 6—Fort Lauderdale to Southampton
The final leg of 3,818 nautical miles began on May 5, 1990.

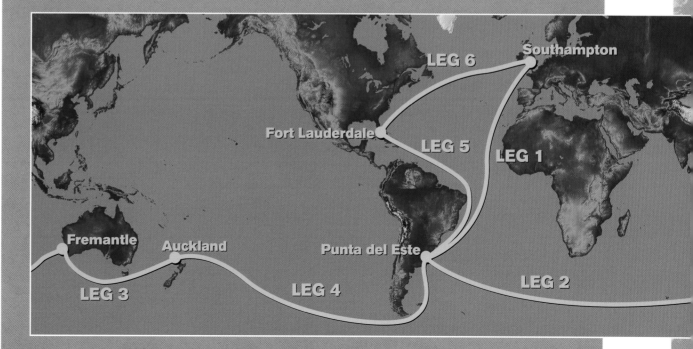

Race Six
1993–1994

It is not commonly known that New Zealand Endeavour *was the only yacht in the Whitbread fleet that didn't change its crew during the race and that it was the only true national entry in the race. The strength of that team ruled supreme.*

Grant Dalton, The Skipper's Log

When Dawn Riley took over as skipper of Heineken, *the boat came alive.*

1993–1994

Although one of our major competitors had gone, which would obviously improve out prospects of winning, the maxi fleet has diminished in stature both in numbers and profile with the demise of Fortuna. The battle between the maxi and the Whitbread 60s for media attention was to become hard-fought throughout the rest of the race, with some of the smaller-boat skippers frequently making reference to the diminished size of the maxi fleet.

Glen Sowry and Grant Dalton on Maxis vs. W60s, Endeavour Winning the Whitbread

This was a two-class race with world champion match racers fighting it out around the world on Whitbread 60s, but Grant Dalton on the maxi *New Zealand Endeavour* taking home the prize. *Yamaha* was the winner in the W60 class.

The start of the sixth Whitbread saw match racing greats Dennis Conner and Chris Dickson, both relatively new to blue water, crossing the starting line for this 32,000-mile thrash on board *Winston* and *Tokio*, two of the 10 newly-designed Whitbread 60 class. Additionally, there were four maxis competing, all but one of them built specifically for this race.

Things had changed considerably in the four years since Peter Blake had set round-the-world records with his win on the maxi *Steinlager 2*. This Whitbread was now a flat-out professional yacht racing effort. All boats were able to obtain corporate sponsorship. Sponsors liked the onboard com-

Every hull received a thorough inspection in Fremantle.

munications coming from the boats while they were racing. Interest levels in the race were high, and building, now that there would be radio communication possible, as well as extensive worldwide television coverage. This would involve many more armchair spectators internationally, and heighten the competition.

Some things were comfortingly the same. Whitbread's venerated veterans Lawrie Smith (on Spain's *Fortuna* for one leg, then on Europe's *Intrum Justitia* for the rest); Grant Dalton (on *New Zealand Endeavour*); Ross Field (on the Japan/New Zealand combined effort, *Yamaha*); Pierre Fehlmann (on the Swiss *Merit Cup*); and Eric Taberly (taking over on leg three on France's *La Poste*) were back as skippers. Experienced crew and recent America's Cup participant, Dawn Riley, had ascended to skipper *Heineken*, formerly *US Women's Challenge*. This race had officially become a lodestar for ambitious

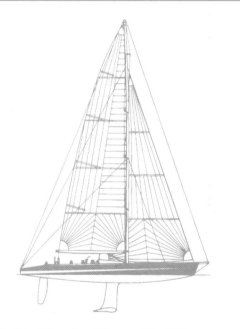

Profile of Yamaha—Winner of the W60 class of the 1993–1994 Whitbread Round The World Race

Skipper—Ross Field, New Zealand
Designer—Farr Yacht Design, New Zealand
LOA—64 feet/19.5 meters
Beam—17.25 feet/5.25 meters
Displacement—30,000 pounds/13,615 kilograms

The compass is a mariner's best friend.

New Zealand Endeavour *features a clipper bow to extend the boat's sail area. The 80-foot maxi was still faster than the new Whitbread 60 class, but not by much.*

sailors, men and women, both as skippers and certainly as crew, worldwide.

On September 25, 1993, the fleet was off on an amended course: leg two now required them to leave Prince Edward Island in the Roaring Forties to starboard, a move the Race Committee hoped would keep the fleet out of the worst of the ice. Still sailed under the Royal Navy Sailing Association flag, the IOR rules applied only to the maxi class, with the Whitbread 60s making up the rest of the fleet. Of the 15 boats at the start, three of the maxis and eight of the 60s were Farr Yacht Design boats.

The fleet saw strong winds astern almost immediately and the W60s piled on the sail. So did Lawrie Smith on the Spanish maxi *Fortuna*, as the boat had been re-rigged as a ketch and could carry almost 100 square meters more sail than the competition. But the load proved too much. *Fortuna's* mizzen failed, followed 2 days later by the rest of the rig. *Fortuna* withdrew, leaving Lawrie Smith available next leg to accept skipper's position on *Intrum Justitia*.

The competitors arrived in Punta del Este within a 4-day window, having sped across the Atlantic except for the obligatory purgatory of the Doldrums. Both *New Zealand Endeavour* and *Tokio* broke Blake's

record, arriving in Punta del Este in 24 days, 7 hours, and 24 days, 10 hours, respectively.

From Punta del Este, the fleet faced one of the most daunting legs of the race: the long haul through the Southern Ocean to Fremantle, Western Australia. With Prince Edward Island a required mark of the course at 46 south latitude, and a little more than half way along the 7,558-nautical-mile leg, the fleet remained surprisingly close. Grant Dalton on *New*

Zealand Endeavour held the lead, with *Tokio* hotfooting it close behind. The W60s were proving to be excellent, if perpetually wet, Southern Ocean racers. It was freezing, it was blowing, and the seas were enormous. Bowmen were plucked off both *Tokio* and *New Zealand Endeavour*. Ken Hara on *Tokio* was retrieved quickly thanks to daylight, good seamanship, EPIRB, and GPS. Craig Watson was clipped onto *New Zealand Endeavour*, and after a minute of being

Punta del Este   CapeTown   Fremantle   Auckland

40° S   Hobart

ROARING FORTIES

Cape Horn   Icebergs   Icebergs

In heavy winds the helmsman wears a safety harness, gloves, and hood. It takes a lot of stamina to steer for extended periods of time.

After 30,000 miles of sailing, the crew of Tokio makes this sail change look easy in 40 knots of wind.

During leg five the entire mast on Tokio had collapsed and was dragging in the water. The crew quickly collected the pieces, jury-rigged a sail, and headed for the nearby port of Santos, Brazil. Once ashore they set to work, and over the next 36 hours constructed a new mast from pieces of the old one, then were back at sea.

A crew member is about to be hoisted aloft.

Intrum Justitia was first to finish, the first of four W60s to beat the first maxi in, Pierre Fehlmann on *Merit Cup. Intrum Justitia* also beat Peter Blake's record for this leg, even with the added 240 miles to accommodate the Prince Edward Islands, by 39 hours.

The respite of Fremantle was much appreciated by the entire fleet. Repairs were made, and some crews changed as well. Eric Taberly was installed as *La Poste's* skipper. Performance was key, and with large sums of money being expended, "investors" wanted good return on their investments.

The 3,272-mile, fairly straightforward leg to Auckland would be a contest between maxi and W60 once again, with the added spice of two New Zealanders vying for first-place homeport honors. Dickson and Dalton battled it out in light air under

Grant Dalton was happy with his team's performance.

the lights in Auckland Harbor with tens of thousands of New Zealanders having stayed up until 3 a.m. to see the duel. *New Zealand Endeavour* crossed first by 3 minutes, much to the disgust of *Tokio's* Dickson, who apologized later for remarks he made under the immediate sting of defeat. Dickson had beaten the other W60s handily, and *New Zealand Endeavour* maintained the maxi lead.

The start from Auckland was confused, with many of the boats having to re-start. All boats found plenty of breeze on this leg, resulting in a succession of broken records: *Yamaha* broke *Intrum Justitia's*, logging 427 miles in 24 hours, but then *Intrum* recouped by logging 428 miles in 24 hours.

New Zealand Endeavour rounded the dreaded Cape Horn first in lovely weather; with *Tokio* just 3 miles behind and *Yamaha* close astern. Past the Falklands *Intrum Justitia* steamed into the lead, then sailed into a hole that *New Zealand Endeavour* man-

dragged through freezing waters, was hauled aboard, also in daylight. It was par for the course as the fleet made its way through the Roaring Forties and the Furious Fifties.

Dalton tried to power up *New Zealand Endeavour* in an effort to put some water between him and the W60s close behind. He added more sail, but when a broach wrecked the mizzen, Dalton knew he had little chance of winning the leg. Lawrie Smith decided to take a chance and head south, looking for better winds. He found them. *Intrum* clocked over 425 miles in one day, a new Whitbread and monohull record.

1993–1994 Results

Position	Yacht	Nationality	Skipper	Elapsed Time
Maxi Class				
1	New Zealand Endeavour	New Zealand	Grant Dalton	120 days 5 hours
2	Merit Cup	Switzerland	Pierre Fehlmann	121 days 2 hours
3	La Poste	France	Eric Tabarly	123 days 22 hours
4	Uruguay Natural	Uruguay	Gustavo Vanzini	144 days 20 hours
Whitbread 60 Class				
1	Yamaha	Japan	Ross Field	120 days 14 hours
2	Intrum Justitia	Europe	Lawrie Smith	121 days 5 hours
3	Galicia '93 Pescanova	Spain	Javier Gandara	122 days 6 hours
4	Winston	USA	Brad Butterworth	122 days 9 hours
5	Tokio	Japan	Chris Dickson	128 days 16 hours
6	Brooksfield	Italy	Guido Maisto	130 days 4 hours
7	Hetman Sahaidachny	Ukraine	Eugene Platon	135 days 23 hours
8	Dolphin & Youth	United Kingdom	Matt Humphries	137 days 21 hours
9	Heineken	USA	Dawn Riley	138 days 16 hours
10	Odessa	Ukraine	Anatoly Verba	158 days 4 hours

A young Knut Frostad looks warily ahead at icebergs aboard Intrum Justitia.

right into the Caribbean Trades. The maxis could ghost through the Doldrums more easily than the W60s, but not quickly enough to pass *Yamaha* who arrived in Ft Lauderdale 7 hours ahead of *Merit Cup*, and 14 hours ahead of *Intrum Justitia*, who never recovered from her time spent parked in the Doldrums. A discouraged Chris Dickson on the repaired *Tokio* finished 9 days after *Yamaha*, and was given much approbation for doing so.

The last leg of this race was important to Grant Dalton on *New Zealand Endeavour* for two reasons: he wanted to beat the round-the-world record, and he was determined to beat the W60s. With *Tokio* out of the running, the battle in the W60s was between *Intrum Justitia* and *Yamaha*.

As the fleet drifted east on the Gulf Stream, they were caught by gales out of the west. Spinnakers went up, and they were off, seeing peak speeds of 25 knots. The W60s beat the maxis on this segment. Far enough north to beware of icebergs, the weather went from bad to worse: the fog was blown away by a 50-knot gale, further punishing the tired boats and weary crews. The strong winds continued right up to the finish, and gave Chris Dickson a thrilling ride. *Tokio* made

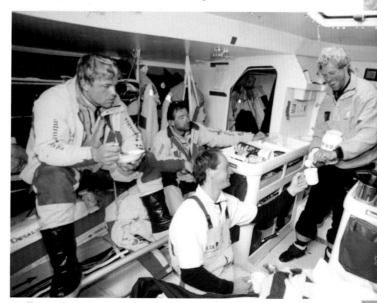

Coffee is always a happy reward for the off watch.

aged to avoid, allowing Dalton to beat Smith into Punta del Este by a scant 5 minutes. Once again he beat *Steinlager 2's* record, this time by 42 hours. At a press conference, Lawrie Smith groused about the maxis in the race. He was all for the W60s and thought the maxis were just in the way.

The race so far had been surprisingly on the wind, with less than a quarter of the race spent running. Consequently, the boats had undergone severe structural stress due to extended and emphatic pounding. Delaminations of the bow sections as well as rudder woes were the diseases of this race, on the leg to Fort

Lauderdale especially, although the more usual and expected rigging problems also cropped up.

Chris Dickson's *Tokio*, with a large overall lead in the W60 class, lost her mast and had to put into Brazil. *La Poste* suffered delamination on her starboard side, and *Heineken* had a myriad of problems. *New Zealand Endeavour* did not escape: delamination on board was repaired by dismantling bunk pipes to use as braces.

The W60 fleet as a whole enjoyed good wind up to the stop light of the Doldrums. Except for *Yamaha*. She found a course that carried her at a steady 10 knots, 120 miles off the Brazilian coast,

126 miles in six hours, a sustained average of 21 knots. Not enough to make up for her standing due to the fifth leg dismasting, but his determination to show the value of the W60 over the maxi as a Whitbread competitor certainly added to his satisfaction as he won the last leg. *Winston* crossed next, followed by *Yamaha* and then *New Zealand Endeavour*. These boats finished within three and a half hours of each other!

Yamaha won the W60 class, and *New Zealand Endeavour* won the maxi class, and the overall time honors. Dalton hadn't beaten the W60s into Southampton, but he had taken 8 days off Peter Blake's *Steinlager 2* round-the-world record, despite

Intrum Justitia set a 24-hour record on leg four of 428 miles in 24 hours.

Whitbread fleet tuning up in the 1993 Fastnet Race.

the fact that *New Zealand Endeavour's* course had been longer than that of *Steinlager 2*.

And even with this win for the maxi supporters, it was the last time even their greatly reduced amenities would grace the Whitbread Round The World Race. Next time it would be all W60s, paired down—it would be about speed, all the time.

Dalton told reporters that his record-breaking circumnavigation proved the Maxis to be the better boat for this race. But 3 years later would find Dalton in the Whitbread Race again, and at the helm of a W60.

Three-sail reaching in heavy conditions----New Zealand Endeavour at 21 knots.

Race course for the sixth Whitbread Round The World Race 1993–1994

Leg 1—Southampton to Punta del Este

Leg 2—Punta del Este to Fremantle

Leg 3—Fremantle to Auckland

Leg 4—Auckland to Punta del Este

Leg 5—Punta del Este to Ft. Lauderdale

Leg 6—Ft. Lauderdale to Southampton

31,975 miles

Leg 1—Southampton to Punta del Este
The fleet left Southampton on September 25, 1993, for this first leg of 5,938 nautical miles.

Leg 2—Punta del Este to Fremantle
The 7,558-nautical-mile leg began on November 13, 1993.

Leg 3—Fremantle to Auckland
The boats departed Fremantle for the 3,272-nautical-mile leg on January 8, 1994.

Leg 4—Auckland to Punta del Este
This leg, covering 5,914 nautical miles, left Auckland on February 19, 1994.

Leg 5—Punta del Este to Fort Lauderdale
Setting sail on April 2, 1994, leg five entailed 5,475 nautical miles.

Leg 6—Fort Lauderdale to Southampton
The final leg of 3,818 nautical miles began on May 21, 1994.

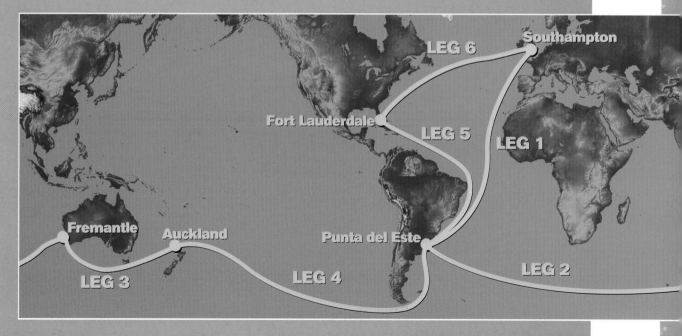

Race Seven
1997–1998

Weren't you scared?
I am often asked.
Yes, I was. Many times.
And that's fine . . .

Knut Frostad,
Responsible for the Irresponsible

Merit Cup *bucks into Auckland first to the delight of her 12 crew, 10 of whom were from New Zealand.*

1997–1998

More America's Cup skippers move their match racing skills onto blue water as the Whitbread 60 class claims the race for its own, and the race becomes all racing, all the time, with the departure of even the minimally comfortable maxi class.

There would be only one class competing in the seventh Whitbread Race. The Whitbread 60 class had proved to be faster and more affordable than the maxi class. The W60s were still the subject of some controversy, as many continued to suggest they were not strong enough to withstand the rigors of racing around the world.

Television coverage, aided by satellite communications advances, combined with the ubiquitous e-mail, would bring this race into more homes than had ever before been possible. Paul Cayard aboard *EF Language* took the lead, providing armchair racers with detailed and clear insight into life aboard a W60.

One important effect of the W60 was its attraction to big-name, round-the-buoys racers. The boat provided a challenge and excitement they could not resist. Dennis Conner was once again trying his skill, as was Chris Dickson. Perhaps the biggest surprise was Paul Cayard, whose bona fides as a Star boat champion and America's Cup competitor hardly seemed to suit the rigors of ocean racing. Some did not take him seriously.

Preparation was as intense as for any other professional sporting contest. Gone were the last-minute efforts. Details relating to hull design and rig were minuscule. And weight became an obsession. Crews had to cut toothbrush handles in half and leave seats off toilets to reduce ounces on these sensitive boats. Food was strictly and scientifically apportioned. No unnecessary gear was allowed. There were no books for recreational reading because the crews of the Whitbread 60s would be racing every second of every day. This was an entirely professionally crewed race, with no unsponsored boats. George Collins, skipper of *Chessie Racing*, was the only amateur. Given the ability to know where all competitors were almost every minute in real time, this was going to be a 31,600-mile match race of fleet proportions.

The September 21, 1997 start was tense. Amid thousands of spectators, Dennis Conner on *Toshiba* had a little run-in with a press boat. After that, the fleet had an easy run down the Solent, with *EF Language* taking an early lead. The winds, as the fleet dropped south, provided the usual mix of brisk/exhilarating

September 21, 1997: Innovation Kvaerner *tears her spinnaker just after the start of leg one off the Cowes, Isle of Wight, England.*

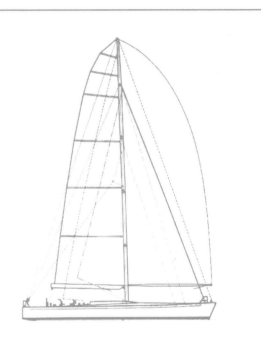

Profile of the Whitbread 60 yacht EF Language

Skipper—Paul Cayard, USA
Designer—Farr Yacht Design, New Zealand
Builder—Richard Gilles & Tim Smythe, Göteborg
LOA—64 feet/19.5 meters
Beam—17.5 feet/5.25 meters
Displacement—30,000 pounds/13,615 kilograms

Looking down on the Swedish Whitbread 60 EF Education *on a three-sail reach.*

October 24, 1997. Swedish Match *nears the end of leg one as she heads toward Cape Town.*

and fluky/light, only to be erased by the great equalizer, the Doldrums. Identifying advantageous weather possibilities and acting on them put *EF Language* ahead of *Innovation Kvaerner*.

The light and fluky winds for much of this leg extended it beyond expectations. Food became problematic and rationing was necessary on some of the boats that had been weight-conscious to the point of allowing only enough food for exactly 31 days (by Race Committee estimates).

Dwindling food supplies increased all boats' interest in getting to Cape Town fast: Lawrie Smith on *Silk Cut* reported a 417.2 mile run on Day 28. Battling close at hand, Grant Dalton hoisted more sail on *Merit Cup*, to recapture second from *Innovation Kvaerner*. Dalton reported that the crew did not sleep for 24 hours. All hands were on deck all the time and racing hard, trying to keep ahead of *Innovation* and catch *EF Language*.

But Cayard and crew crossed the line first, 29 days, 16 hours, and 54 minutes after the start. The win was solid: *Merit Cup* finished second 20 hours later, and within 2 more hours *Innovation Kvaerner* was in.

Ashore, *Toshiba* announced that Chris Dickson had resigned, replaced by four-time Whitbread veteran and *Toshiba* watch captain, Paul Standbridge. Then it was announced that *America's Challenge* was retiring entirely due to lack of funding, leaving Ross Field, winner of the last Whitbread, and his ace crew without a ride. *America's Challenge* had been one of just two W60s not designed by Farr Yacht Design, and the crew had been impressed with her ability, so was doubly disappointed.

With Dickson gone, Field out of contention, and Cayard's unexpectedly brilliant showing, suddenly *EF Language* was the co-favorite with *Merit Cup*. *Silk Cut* and *Innovation Kvaerner* shared second favorite, and *Toshiba* with new skipper Paul Standbridge had slipped to a solid third.

Leaving Cape Town on November 8, 1997, the fleet stuck close to shore, except for *Swedish Match*. Gunnar Krantz acted on his co-skipper's observation that the smoke from the stack of a freighter far out to sea

seemed to indicate fresh breeze, and they daringly peeled off and found 10 steady knots of wind at sea, while the fleet hugging the shore drifted in less than a knot. As *Swedish Match* opened up more than a 100-mile spread among the fleet, Cayard was humbled.

Beyond Prince Edward Island at the end of day six, the Roaring Forties hit with full force. *Swedish Match* reported a 420.6-mile day.

As the rest of the fleet hit the notorious winds and miserable sea conditions of the Roaring Forties, damage reports started coming in: *Chessie Racing* hit a

The Southern Ocean Experience

Then we hit the back of a wave with a surge of deceleration. Tons of water threw itself aft down the deck and I felt my knees load up as I was pushed into the bulkhead . . . My stomach was in my mouth and my back lifting off the bunk as the boat dropped, airborne, into the next trough. The rollercoaster ride from hell.

Magnus Olsson, EF Language

Above: On the bow of EF Language *during leg two from Cape Town, South Africa, to Fremantle, Australia. The bowman appears to be surfing through the water. Where is the boat?*

Right: November 14, 1997. Crew members reach for something solid onboard Whitbread 60 yacht Merit Cup *as she broaches during the second leg from Cape Town, South Africa to Fremantle, Australia.*

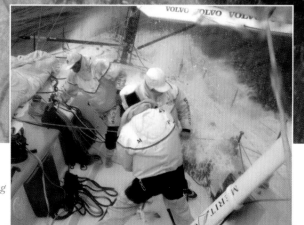

whale, taking a 4-foot section out of the keel. Lawrie Smith reported that his boat, surfing down a steep wave at 25 knots with a 32-knot wind astern, buried its bow in the wave trough and sent a solid wall of water roiling down the deck, pushing full sail bags with force in front of it, taking out every stanchion.

But *Swedish Match* powered on, one day averaging just over 18 knots for 12 hours. Cayard, frustrated, pushed *EF Language* to the max, reporting on day 12 that he was making 20 knots in 30 knots of wind. He was candid in his report: "The boat is shuddering, shaking, slamming, and generally just in a state of violence." On deck, he said it was just plain freezing. Day 13 gave

September 21, 1997. General view of the start of leg one from Southampton to Cape Town. Boats shown in the Solent off the Isle of Wight, England. The spectator fleet always wants to speed ahead of the racing boats. It is like they are in the race too.

Lines are color coded to keep track of their function.

Silk Cut a new record: 449.1 miles in 24 hours, an average of 18.8 knots. Later that same day, she averaged a fabulous 19.4 knots in 6 hours, giving *EF Language* a serious challenge.

Cayard responded by taxing the boat and crew seemingly to the limits, as the overpowered boat broached in gale force winds. But the W60s seemed up to the harsh conditions, the crews impervious to the miserable degradations, and while there was damage everywhere, neither boats nor crew were seriously injured.

Serenely ahead on day 15, *Swedish Match* was undeniably going to win the leg, beating second-to-finish *Innovation Kvaerner* by 19 hours. *Toshiba* finished the next day, followed by *Silk Cut*. *EF Language* finished a humbling fifth.

The crews—and the boats—arriving in Fremantle looked as if they had been at sea for 20 weeks instead of under 20 days. This 4,600-nautical-mile leg of the Southern Ocean had lived up to its reputation, with winds astern pushing the boats mercilessly through the awful, frigid sea conditions. *Swedish Match* gained the glory of having accomplished the fastest average speed on any Whitbread leg: 13 knots. Lawrie Smith on *Silk Cut* broke the previous world monohull record by 15 miles, logging 449.1 miles in 24 hours, an average of 18.7 knots.

On December 13, 1997, the fleet set out for Sydney, a 2,250-mile leg that would end with a spectacular finish, the tightest imaginable. Six boats crossed

The Whitbread is more than just a nine-legged race, or a series of nine races. It is a series of 6-hour races. In these very fickle and flukey winds, we find ourselves on the edges of our seats at every sked wondering if the others have been as slow as we.

Paul Cayard, EF Language

Packs of dehydrated food.

We were very extreme about food on leg one. We cut it way too short. As a crew we lost about 10% of our body weight. Food is weight, obviously, which is detrimental. So we were on very light rations . . . We learned a hard lesson. On subsequent legs, we would double the portions we served for lunch and dinner . . .

Paul Cayard, EF Language

the line within 11 minutes, and all nine boats finished within 2 hours. *EF Language* had beaten an injured *Swedish Match* by 5 minutes and 8 seconds. Fifty-three seconds later, *Chessie Racing* crossed the line, then 2 minutes, 16 seconds later *Merit Cup* crossed. One minute 41 seconds later *Innovation Kvaerner* finished, followed 46 seconds later by *Toshiba*. It was unprecedentedly exciting for crews and spectators alike.

It had taken EF *Language* 9 days, 9 hours, and 9 minutes to win the leg, and Cayard was cranked. Not only had they won an impossibly close finish, but he had expiated his performance in the second leg: *EF Language* was back in first place.

Christmas and the New Year in Sydney provided but a brief respite for the crews. Much work was to be done on all boats before the January 4, 1998, start for Auckland. Masts were the objects of most fixes.

The boats were able to fly their Code 0 sails as they started from Sydney Harbor and made for Auckland. Co-invented by Lawrie Smith and Paul Cayard, these are masthead, gennaker-like sails with loose luffs that are extremely effective going upwind in light air.

Swedish Match was first to pass Cape Reinga, and promptly fell into a windless hole. As the fleet rounded the Cape, they saw her sitting idle in front of them and were thus able to avoid the same fate. *Merit Cup*, with her crew of Kiwis,

Onboard Innovation Kvaerner *during the second leg. The view from down below.*

determinedly passed *Toshiba* and made for the finish. Grant Dalton totally enjoyed being first into his homeport. *Toshiba* and *Merit Cup* match raced to the line in 45 knots of wind, with spectators lining the shore for miles. Conner and Dalton raced through lumpy seas and an enormous spectator fleet, with Dalton crossing just 2 minutes and 36 seconds ahead of Conner. As Dalton crossed, a strong gust blew her mainsail to shreds. Two Whitbreads in a row, 4 years apart, Dalton was once again the hero of his country, by being first into Auckland. Again the majority of the fleet finished within 3 hours, with *BrunelSunergy* and *EF Education* bringing up the rear.

Preparations for the next leg, the potentially dangerous 6,670-nautical-mile thrash around Cape Horn to the new South American port of call, Saõ Sebastio, Brazil, were intense. The Whitbread 60s had made it through their first taste of the Southern Ocean with minimal damage, but they had logged over 15,000 nautical miles on their sea-going odometers, and with a little more than that still to go, the second dip into the Southern Ocean was not something to take lightly.

The start took place amidst cheering crowds and with a light breeze filling spinnakers. Soon even that slight wind died, leaving the boats anticlimactically drifting away from Auckland. The slow sailing was frustrating for days.

Then the leaders of the fleet found wind—a strengthening 30-knot easterly: they were pounding right into it, while the back of the pack was running before 45 knots of westerly breeze. In the lead, *EF Language* was first to sight an iceberg, estimated at a mile long, and heralding worsening weather. Weight on these boats was always critical to performance, but navigator Mark Rudiger didn't dare leave his nav station for fear of lightening the stern sufficiently to bury the bow in the oncoming waves. Conditions aboard could not have been pleasant.

EF Language was in high cotton, 350 miles ahead of *Swedish Match, Toshiba, Merit Cup,* and *Innovation*

Kvaerner, having sailed around Cape Horn in a strong and favorable wind that deserted the rest of the fleet. Everyone else was barely ghosting along, and getting mighty peevish about it, too.

Behind those four, Roy Heiner on *BrunelSunergy* decided to avoid the parking lot he saw ahead, and turned decidedly east, a risky strategy leaving the Fauklands to port. That paid off: he found steady 25-knot winds while the other four boats continued to float haplessly along. Seventh place *Chessie Racing* benefitted from being able to judge the progress—or lack of it—ahead. While Heiner made out by sailing so far east, passing all four stopped boats, *Chessie* chose a more moderate but still easterly course and managed to fall in behind *BrunelSunergy* as the winds finally came to the other four boats. Strong currents hindered the westerly boats as well, and *EF Language* crossed 3 days ahead of *BrunelSunergy*, followed by

Position	Yacht	Flag	Skipper(s)	Points
	1997–1998 Results			
1	EF Language	Sweden	Paul Cayard	836
2	Merit Cup	Monaco	Grant Dalton	698
3	Swedish Match	Sweden	Gunnar Krantz	689
4	Innovation Kvaerner	Norway	Knut Frostad	633
5	Silk Cut	United Kingdom	Lawrie Smith	630
6	Chessie Racing	United States	George Collins	613
7	Toshiba	United States	Dennis Conner, Paul Standbridge	528
8	BrunelSunergy	Netherlands	Hans Bouscholte, Roy Heiner	415
9	EF Education	Sweden	Christine Guillou	275
DNF	America's Challenge	United States	Ross Field	48

Chessie Racing's third, third-place finish.

Silk Cut had retired from the leg and motored to Ushuaia, Argentina to replace her broken mast. *EF Education* seemed to be plagued by gear failure. A broken shroud put her mast at risk, and while limping into Ushuaia for repairs, battered by 35-knott winds, the mast snapped above the first set of spreaders. Once in Ushuaia, the mast was replaced, and they continued on. After 2 light days, they suffered a gale that blew out their patched-up mainsail. The women realized that if they didn't cut their losses and motor on to Saõ Sebastião, they wouldn't make the start of the next leg. Their determination, their demonstrated ability, and their amazingly even tempers made them a much-appreciated entry no matter their place in the finish order

Ashore, things had heated up for *Toshiba*. She was accused of motoring without proper notification of race committee or documentation. Her engine had been turned on, the seal on it broken, reportedly to clear kelp that had been unusually heavy near Cape Horn. But no records were kept, and so *Toshiba* was disqualified from that leg, dropping her from fifth overall to sixth.

The start of leg six was a mess, purely and simply. Spectators crammed on anything that floated, cluttering the starting area, causing turmoil of sea and confusion without sufficient winds to push the W60s clear. Finally, just south of Ilha Bela, the wind picked up from the southwest at 28 knots and the fleet sprouted fractional spinnakers and were off on a lively reach.

Getting through the Doldrums didn't take the fleet long, but the alternating calm/vicious squall

Skipper Dennis Conner of the United States slams a reefed Toshiba *into Auckland to finish second in the fourth leg.*

Match finished, followed by *Innovation Kvaerner* and then *Merit Cup*. *EF Language* seemed to have the race well within her grasp.

The stopover in Fort Lauderdale allowed Dennis Conner to reclaim *Toshiba's* helm, and all the crews to contemplate the 870-mile dash up the east coast of the United States to Baltimore, Maryland. The last 130 miles would be tight racing within the shallow confines of the Chesapeake Bay.

But first the fleet had to get to the mouth of the Bay, and that meant riding the Gulf Stream north. This proved a boat-slamming tactic, as the current flowed against 20 to 25-knot headwinds, creating an unbelievable chop. *BrunelSunergy* chose a radical course much farther east, in search of both better winds and flatter seas, and that paid off. But *Swedish Match* came on as they approached the mouth of the Bay, as did *EF Language*. By the next morning, Cayard was 11 miles behind Heiner, with a tiny lead on Krantz. *EF Language* fought hard to stay ahead of *Swedish Match*, while *BrunelSunergy* caught a 10-knot following breeze to finish under spinnaker at 5 p.m., April 22. Cayard fought to the very end, forcing jibes every 60 to 90 seconds, but *Swedish Match* prevailed, selecting a better headsail for the wind shift that occurred and crossing the line a mere 30 seconds before *EF Language*, and 21 minutes after *BrunelSunergy*.

To the delight of the many spectators, fierce battles were being waged as the rest of the fleet came up the Bay. *Innovation Kvaerner* finished just 3 minutes before *Silk Cut*, and the closest finish in Whitbread history was the incredible 10 seconds that separated *Toshiba* and *Chessie Racing*. *EF Education* finished 2 hours later, and as soon as skipper Christine Guillou stepped ashore, she filed a protest against *Toshiba*, with *EF Education* claiming that Conner's *Toshiba* had sailed recklessly in a port/starboard confrontation. The International Jury penalized *Toshiba* two places on the leg, which meant she was in last place.

The official site of the leg seven stopover was shared between the cities of Baltimore and Annapolis. While the finish had been at Baltimore, the start of leg eight

Preparations for the start of leg five in Auckland.

weather pattern was a trial to all. And the incessant heat, combined with the continuous damp conditions, produced a series of heat rash and fungal infestations for all the crews. The W60s had to be sailed every second, so there was no time for airing clothing or bodies. Conditions known not so fondly as "gunwale bum" or "spotty botty" were prevalent.

Silk Cut was first to finish in Fort Lauderdale, 4 days earlier than anticipated, and little more than an hour before *EF Language*. Four hours later, *Swedish*

Richard Bouzaid of New Zealand concentrates at the helm as his countryman Nick Willetts trims the mainsail during the fifth leg from Auckland to Saõ Sebastião aboard Innovation Kvaerner.

Helming on a knife edge without hat or gloves in the Southern Ocean onboard BrunelSunergy *during the fifth leg.*

With four-time America's Cup winner Dennis Conner at the helm, Toshiba *clearly takes the start of leg seven off Fort Lauderdale on the way to Baltimore.*

60s were capable of covering the 450 miles in little better than a day, there was no time for subtle strategy. All boats were raced all-out, and positions changed constantly.

With just 75 nautical miles to go, the Race Committee inserted a 25-mile detour to allow the boats to finish with the pre-arranged fanfare. The fleet had been too quick, and the press and spectators weren't expecting them until afternoon. This also meant that the leaders would be sailing up the Solent at slack tide. Those at the end of the pack would have a serious current to buck. Each boat had as much sail up as possible, and things broke and were fixed as the fleet pounded into headwinds and against the tide. Grant Dalton on *Merit Cup* (second overall) barely beat *EF Language* across the line, *Innovation Kvaerner* crossed third, *Silk Cut* fourth, and *Swedish Match* (third overall), having had to deal with even the small distraction of a blown-out mainsail, finished fifth.

would take place off Annapolis, the "sailing capital of the United States," so the fleet moved south in a much fêted parade of boats on April 30.

The start itself took place just north of the Chesapeake Bay Bridge, on the same day, at the same time, as an annual charitable "bridge walk" in which 50,000 people took part. The Bay itself was lined with approximately 6,000 well-behaved spectator craft, sometimes in ranks five deep. With the bridge blocking the light winds, the boats struggled through the start and down the Bay.

The crossing was not uneventful: *Merit Cup* caught a dead seal on her keel strut, struck a whale, and was struck by a dolphin, causing further rudder damage. She finished fifth. *Toshiba* and *Silk Cut* battled for first, *Toshiba* taking line honors in La Rochelle, France, just 10 minutes ahead. *Chessie Racing* logged their fourth, third-place finish, and *EF Education* enjoyed her

best leg, finishing fourth under the guidance of Isabelle Autissier, renowned single-handed skipper. *Swedish Match* lost to *EF Language*, effectively conceding the race to Cayard and crew.

The 450-mile jaunt back to Southampton was where second and third places would be decided. *EF Language* had the overall trophy won even if they didn't start the final leg, putting paid to those who had disparaged Cayard as a skipper 9 months previously. For second place, the contest would be between *Swedish Match*, *Merit Cup*, and *Chessie Racing*. Lawrie Smith on *Silk Cut* was in a good place to capture third . . . unless one of the other boats got in the way. It was to be a serious, hard-fought contest on this last leg of the 32,600-mile race.

The start was contentious as the starting gun misfired, but the fleet was off and racing hard, and since the Whitbread

Paul Cayard, skipper of the winning yacht, EF Language.

The crew onboard EF Language *hoist their Code 0 at the start of the fifth leg.*

The race over, exhausted skippers retracted all protests centering on the start of the final leg. The W60s had made it around the world, and the baton would be handed from the Whitbread Company to AB Volvo, who would own and sponsor the next race in 2001.

The skipper navigator partnership is really key in the Whitbread. It's always important, but unlike the America's Cup, on the Whitbread you don't go home after racing and get closed off from your partner for 12 hours. It's "on" full time. And Mark and I are quite different. I'm more high-strung, more Type A. He's very low key . . . he provides a good balance for me . . . when there's a problem, the crew wakes both of us.

Paul Cayard, EF Language

EF Language *crosses the Channel during the final leg of the Whitbread Round The World Race.*

Race course for the seventh Whitbread Round The World Race 1997–1998

Leg 1—Southampton to Cape Town

Leg 2—Cape Town to Fremantle

Leg 3—Fremantle to Sydney

Leg 4—Sydney to Auckland

Leg 5—Auckland to Saõ Sebastião

Leg 6—Saõ Sebastião to Fort Lauderdale

Leg 7—Fort Lauderdale to Baltimore

Leg 8—Annapolis to La Rochelle

Leg 9—La Rochelle to Southampton

31,600 miles

Leg 1—Southampton to Cape Town
The fleet set off on September 21, 1997, for Cape Town, a distance of 7,350 nautical miles.

Leg 2—Cape Town to Fremantle
Leg two began on November 11, 1997. This Southern Ocean crossing covered a distance of 4,600 nautical miles.

Leg 3—Fremantle to Sydney
The 2,250-nautical-mile leg began in Fremantle on December 13, 1997.

Leg 4—Sydney to Auckland
The short hop to Auckland of 1,270 nautical miles left on January 4, 1998.

Leg 5—Auckland to Saõ Sebastião
The second Southern Ocean leg of the race, 6,670 nautical miles, began on February 1, 1998.

Leg 6—Saõ Sebastião to Fort Lauderdale
March 14, 1998 was departure date for Fort Lauderdale, 4,750 nautical miles.

Leg 7—Fort Lauderdale to Baltimore
The fleet left for Baltimore on April 19, 1998, a distance of 870 nautical miles.

Leg 8—Annapolis to La Rochelle
The 3,390-nautical-mile-leg began on May 3, 1998.

Leg 9—La Rochelle to Southampton
The ninth and final leg left La Rochelle on May 22, 1998, sailing the last 450 nautical miles.

Part Five
Epilogue

Introduction

The thrilling last leg of the Volvo Ocean Race resembled the finale of a spectacular fireworks display where large aquatic audiences gasped at ever bigger explosions, bursting lights, and surprises. After spending most of the 32,700-mile course racing out of sight of land, the 94 sailors on board the eight V.O.60s were surprised by the enormous support both at the start of the leg in Göteborg and the finish in Kiel.

One day later at the raucous prize giving, all eight teams received standing ovations. The biggest cheers came from the sailors themselves who applauded each other's accomplishments. They were now bonded together for having endured, in fact, thrived in the most physically exhausting and tightly contested race around the world under sail.

The competition was remarkably balanced. After nine legs, seven of the eight boats had podium (top three) finishes. And the all-women's team came close by finishing an impressive fourth on leg nine. *Assa Abloy's* Chris Larson remarked at the prize giving, "The difference on every leg seemed to come down to just one boatlength at a key moment. The problem is you never knew when that moment would occur." The sailors had to be constantly alert. Boats behind could often make up a lot of distance in a short period of time.

For those of us on shore we felt both the pain and the exhilaration through e-mail reports, video clips, and pictures. The sailors found the exercise of communication to be good therapy, knowing that people listened, watched, and cared.

Three million unique visitors logged on to www.volvooceanrace.org, and many millions more watched on television. Thousands of people visited the race villages. In Göteborg and Kiel several hundred thousand were there at the start and the finish.

The 9 months of hard racing took its toll on the sailors, and they were relieved to reach the finish line. Some of their stories were harsh: two broken masts, three broken rudders, health problems, knockdowns, and the nightmare of strategic planning going awry. Other stories were of dreams fulfilled: setting new speed records or prevailing against the odds in tight finishes. And yet every sailor kept fighting all the way to the finish.

illbruck prevailed, thanks to meticulous preparation, innovative sail development, and intense focus by a talented crew. But with fourths on three legs, *illbruck's* crew understood that they were vulnerable. We learned, once again, that the sailor does make a difference, as witnessed by *Assa Abloy's* big turnaround after their skipper change in Cape Town.

In the 1997–98 Whitbread, *EF Language* set a high standard. The lessons learned aboard that boat served both *illbruck* and *Assa Abloy* well. The unsung hero of both *EF Language* and *Assa Abloy* was the affable Magnus Olsson, who masterminded each campaign. *EF Language* skipper Paul Cayard spent the next 2 years sailing with John Kostecki aboard the America's Cup challenger *AmericaOne*. There is no doubt that Kostecki gleaned a lot of valuable information from the time spent with Cayard. *Assa Abloy* also benefited from the talent of American Mark Rudiger, another *EF Language* alumnus.

The overachiever of the fleet was *Amer Sports One*. The boat struggled in waves, but veterans Grant Dalton and Roger Nilson, along with Dee Smith and Bouwe Bekking found a way to finish a respectable third.

At the prizegiving, the always understated Helge Alten thanked the stakeholders, including the 139 sailors who sailed in at least one leg, sponsors, media, race management, jury, ports, and syndicates for making the Volvo Ocean Race successful. Alten mentioned how happy he was that everyone had returned safely. With that comment he received a sustained standing ovation. The Volvo Ocean Race was an enormous logistical challenge. It achieved unprecedented acclaim on the world stage, and in addition to the safety record, the accomplishments were many.

Every boat had a chance to win. The blending of sailing skill and technological innovation created impressive performances, and speed records were broken on three legs. When there were problems, the sailors were resourceful. Perhaps best of all, the racing was amazingly tight, with only minutes separating the boats on most legs. The Volvo Ocean Race round the world truly generated a "fighting finish."

After the ceremony in Kiel, I overheard two sailors talking. "Are you going to do this again?" one asked. "Absolutely, how about you?" "I wouldn't miss it for the world." "For the world?" I thought to myself. Maybe they already own a piece of it, just having sailed around it.

The Boats and the Results

Yacht Name	LEG 1 (Pos)	LEG 2 (Pos)	LEG 3 (Pos)	LEG 4 (Pos)	LEG 5 (Pos)	LEG 6 (Pos)	LEG 7 (Pos)	LEG 8 (Pos)	LEG 9 (Pos)	TOTAL POINTS
illbruck	1	1	4	1	2	4	1	4	2	61
Assa Abloy	5	6	1	4	1	3	2	1	3	55
Amer Sports One	2	5	2	5	6	2	5	5	5	44
Tyco	4	8	3	3	3	6	3	2	7	42
News Corp	3	3	5	6	5	1	6	3	8	41
djuice	7	4	6	2	7	7	7	7	1	33
SEB	6	2	8	8	4	5	4	6	6	32
Amer Sports Too	8	7	7	7	8	8	8	8	4	16

Final Standings

Amer Sports One
Skipper—Grant Dalton
Navigator—Roger Nilson
Designer—Mani Frers

Amer Sports Too
Skipper—Lisa McDonald
Navigators—Genevieve White and Miranda Merron
Designer—Farr Yacht Design

Assa Abloy
Skipper—Neal McDonald
Co-skipper/navigator—Mark Rudiger
Designer—Farr Yacht Design

djuice
Skipper—Knut Frostad
Navigator—Jean-Yves Bernot
Designer—Laurie Davidson

illbruck
Skipper—John Kostecki
Navigator—Juan Vila
Designer—Farr Yacht Design

News Corp
Skipper—Jez Fanstone
Syndicate Head/Navigator—Ross Field
Designer—Farr Yacht Design

SEB
Skipper—Gunnar 'Gurra' Krantz
Navigator—Marcel van Triest
Designer—Farr Yacht Design

Tyco
Skipper—Kevin Shoebridge
Navigator—Steve Hayles
Designer—Farr Yacht Design

Prize Winners

Leg One: Southampton to Cape Town

First	illbruck
Second	Amer Sports One
Third	News Corp
Seamanship Award	Mikeal Lundh (djuice)
Best 24-Hour Run	illbruck—369.9 miles
Best Media Contribution	Peter Dorien (djuice)

Leg Two: Cape Town to Sydney

First	illbruck
Second	SEB
Third	News Corp
Seamanship Award	Roger Nilson (Amer Sports One) & Gareth Cooke (SEB)
Best 24-Hour Run	SEB—460.4 miles
Best Media Contribution	Pepe Ribes Rubio (Amer Sports One)

Leg Three: Sydney to Auckland

First	Assa Abloy
Second	Amer Sports One
Third	Tyco
Seamanship Award	Klabbe Nylof (Assa Abloy)
Best 24-Hour Run	illbruck—327.7 miles
Best Media Contribution	Richard Mason (Assa Abloy)

Leg Four: Auckland to Rio de Janeiro

First	illbruck
Second	djuice
Third	Tyco
Seamanship Award	Katie Pettibone (Amer Sports Too)
Best 24-Hour Run	illbruck—451.8 miles
Best Media Contribution	Ray Davies (illbruck)

Leg Five: Rio de Janeiro to Miami

First	Assa Abloy
Second	illbruck
Third	Tyco
Seamanship Award	Emma Westmacott (Amer Sports Too)
Best 24-Hour Run	illbruck—351.1 miles
Best Media Contribution	Magnus Woxen (SEB)

Leg Six: Miami to Baltimore

First	News Corp
Second	Amer Sports One
Third	Assa Abloy
Seamanship Award	Damien Duke (News Corp)
Best 24-Hour Run	News Corp—294.9 miles
Best Media Contribution	Klaartje Zuiderbaan (Amer Sports Too)

Leg Seven: Annapolis to La Rochelle

First	illbruck
Second	Assa Abloy
Third	Tyco
Seamanship Award	Lisa McDonald (Amer Sports Too)
Best 24-Hour Run	illbruck—481 miles
Best Media Contribution	Keryn Henderson (Amer Sports Too)

Leg Eight: La Rochelle to Göteborg

First	Assa Abloy
Second	Tyco
Third	News Corp
Seamanship Award	Jan Dekker (Tyco)
Best 24-Hour Run	Tyco—326.4 miles
Best Media Contribution	Guy Salter (Tyco)

Leg Nine: Göteborg to Kiel

First	djuice
Second	illbruck
Third	Assa Abloy
Roaring Forties Trophy	illbruck for best aggregate score on Southern Ocean legs
Overall Best 24-Hour Run	illbruck for leg seven
Overall Best Media Contribution	Assa Abloy

Kiel, Germany. NDR Big Band plays before the prizegiving begins.

Crew Lists

Amer Sports One

Grant Dalton, Skipper
Age 44, New Zealand
Experience:
1981–82 *Flyer II*
1985–86 *Lion New Zealand*
1989–90 Skipper *Fisher & Paykel*
1993–94 Skipper *New Zealand Endeavour*
1997–98 Skipper on *Merit Cup*

Bouwe Bekking, Co-skipper/Watch Leader
Age 38, The Netherlands
Experience:
1985–86 *Philips Innovator*
1993–94 *Winston*
1997–98 *Merit Cup*

Roger Nilson, Navigator
Age 56, Sweden
Experience:
1981–82 *Alaska Eagle*
1985–86 *Drum*
1989–90 *The Card*
1993–94 *Intrum Justitia*

Paul Cayard, Watch Captain (leg four only)
Age 42, USA
Experience: 1997–98 Skipper *EF Language*—Winner

Dee Smith, Watch Captain/Tactician (off leg four)
Age 49, USA
Experience: 1997–98 *Chessie Racing*

Peter Pendleton, Yacht Systems
Age 29, USA/Canada

Pepe Ribes Rubio, Bow
Age 30, Spain

Jeff Brock, Bow
Age 33, Canada

Fredrik Loof, Trimmer (leg three onward)
Age 31, Sweden

Keith Kilpatrick, Trimmer (legs one and two only)
Age 40, USA

Chris Nicholson, Helm/Trimmer
Age 32, Australia

Claudio Celon, Trimmer
Age 40, Italy

Phil Airey, Trimmer/Sail Coordinator
Age 33, New Zealand

Stefano Rizzi, Trimmer
Age 33, Italy
Experience: 1993–94 *Brooksfield*

Amer Sports Too

Lisa McDonald, Skipper
Age 31, USA
Experience: 1997–98 *EF Education*

Genevieve White, Navigator (legs one–three)
Age 33, Australia

Miranda Merron, Navigator (leg four onward)
Age 32, United Kingdom

Katie Pettibone, Watch Captain
Age 29, USA
Experience: 1997–98 *EF Education*

Bridget Suckling, Bow (off leg five)
Age 28, New Zealand
Experience: 1997–98 *EF Education*

Emma Westmacott, Watch Captain
Age 33, Australia
Experience: 1997–98 *EF Education*

Abigail Seager, Boat Systems
Age 25, United Kingdom

Keryn Henderson, Foredeck/Helm/Medic
Age 28, New Zealand
Experience: 1997–98 *EF Education*

Eleanor Hay, Pit/Trimmer (legs one, five, and seven)
Age 30, United Kingdom

Anna Drougge, Trimmer/Sail Maker
Age 33, Sweden
Experience: 1997–98 *EF Education*

Amer Sports One *breaks through heavy seas in the early hours of leg eight from La Rochelle to Göteborg.*

Amer Sports Too comes in fourth for leg nine.

Klaartje Zuiderbaan, Trimmer/Helm
Age 28, The Netherlands

Sharon Ferris, Trimmer/Helm (legs one, two, and three)
Age 27, New Zealand

Melissa Purdy, Trimmer/Helm
(legs one, three, five, and six)
Age 32, USA
Experience: 1997–98 *EF Education*

Willemien van Hoeve, Crew
Age 29, The Netherlands

Carolijn Brouwer, Trimmer (legs two and four)
Age 28, The Netherlands

Elizabeth Wardley, Foredeck (leg two onward)
Age 20, Australia

Emma Richards, Trimmer/Helm (legs four and five)
Age 28, United Kingdom

Joanna Burchell, Trimmer (leg six onward)
Age 29, United Kingdom

Christine Briand, Crew (legs eight and nine)
Age 42, France
Experience: 1997–98 *EF Education*

Assa Abloy

Neal McDonald, Helm/Trimmer (leg one only)
   Skipper (leg two onward)
Age 38, United Kingdom
Experience:
1993–94 *Fortuna*
1997–98 *Silk Cut*

Roy Heiner, Skipper (leg one only)
Age 40, The Netherlands
Experience: 1997–98 Skipper *BrunelSunergy*

Mark Rudiger, Co-skipper/Navigator
Age 47, USA
Experience: 1997–98 *EF Language*—Winner

Jason Carrington, Bow (off leg four)
Age 32, United Kingdom
Experience:
1993–94 *Fortuna*
1997–98 *Silk Cut*

Klas Nylôf, Trimmer
Age 34, Sweden
Experience: 1997–98 *EF Language*

Sidney Gavignet, Helm/Trimmer
Age 32, France
Experience: 1993–94 *La Poste*

Mike Joubert, Bow
Age 29, South Africa
Experience: 1997–98 *BrunelSunergy*

Richard Mason, Trimmer/Pit
Age 27, New Zealand

Stu Wilson, Trimmer/Sail Maker
Age 34, New Zealand
Experience:
1993–94 *Fortuna*
1997–98 *Chessie Racing*

Guillermo Altadill, Helm/Trimmer
   (legs one, three, and seven)
Age 39, Spain
Experience:1989–90 *Fortuna*

Chris Larson, Helm/Tactician (leg three onward)
Age 35, USA

Jules Mazars, Helm/Trimmer (off leg seven)
Age 34, France

Magnus Olsson, Helm
Age 52, Sweden
Experience:
1985–86 *Drum*
1989–90 *The Card*
1993–94 *Intrum Justitia*
1997–98 *EF Language*

Roberto Bermudez de Castro, Helmsman/Trimmer
   (legs two and four)
Age 31, Spain
Experience: 1993–94 *Galicia Pescanova*

In the Southern Ocean aboard Assa Abloy, *leg four*

Herve Jan, Helm/Trimmer (leg two only)
Age 44, France
Experience:
1985–86 *Shadow of Switzerland*
1989–90 *Gatorade*
1993–94 *Brooksfield*
1997–98 *BrunelSunergy*

Joshua Alexander, Bow (leg four only)
Age 25, New Zealand

Mike Howard, Trimmer (leg five onward)
Age 51, USA

djuice

Knut Frostad, Skipper
Age 34, Norway
Experience:
1993–94 *Intrum Justitia*
1997–98 Skipper *Innovation Kvaerner*

Jean-Yves Bernot, Navigator (off legs eight and nine)
Age 52, France

Stig Westergaard, Trimmer/Helm (off leg nine)
Age 38, Denmark

Jacques Vincent, Watch Leader
Age 39, France
Experience:
1989–90 *The Card*
1993–94 *Tokio*
1997–98 *Innovation Kvaerner*

Christen Horn Johannessen, Trimmer/Helm
  (leg one only)
Age 34, Norway
Experience: 1997–98 *Innovation Kvaerner*

Espen Guttormsen, Watch Leader (off leg four)
Age 33, Norway
Experience: 1997–98 *Innovation Kvaerner*

Jonas Wackenhuth, Bow
Age 32, Sweden

Peter "Spike" Dorien, Trimmer/Helm (legs one–four)
Age 30, Australia

Wouter Verbraak, Assistant Navigator (legs one and six)
Age 25, The Netherlands

Mikael Lundh, Bow (off leg three)
Age 28, Sweden
Experience: 1997–98 *Swedish Match*

Erle Williams, Tactician (legs three, eight, and nine)
Age 42, New Zealand
Experience: 1997–98 *Swedish Match*

Arve Roaas, Trimmer/Helm (off leg nine)
Age 39, Norway

Anthony Nossiter, Trimmer/Helm
Age 28, Australia

David Blanchfield, Bow (leg three)
Age 34, Australia
Experience: 1997–98 *Toshiba*

Steve Gruver, Trimmer/Helm (legs one–three)
Age 41, USA

Terry Hutchinson, Crew (leg two only)
Age 33, USA

Thomas Colville, Crew (leg four only)
Age 33, France

Peter "Billy" Merrington, Trimmer/Helm (leg four only)
Age 31, Australia

Grant Wharington, Trimmer/Helm (leg four only)
Age 37, Australia

David Jarvis, Sailmaker (legs five–seven)
Age 35, United Kingdom/Canada

Franck Proffit, Trimmer (leg five only)
Age 37, France

Herve Cunningham, Trimmer (leg five onward)
Age 27, France

Jeff Scott, Watch Leader (leg six onward)
Age 37, New Zealand
Experience:
1989–90 *Fisher & Paykel*
1993–94 *Yamaha*
1997–98 *Toshiba*

illbruck

John Kostecki, Skipper
Age 37, USA
Experience: 1997–98 *Chessie Racing*

Juan Vila, Navigator
Age 39, Spain
Experience:
1989–90 *Fortuna Extra Lights*
1993–94 *Galicia-Pescanova*
1997–98 *Chessie Racing*

djuice *plows through the waves at the start of leg two.*

The crew of illbruck *on the rail after the start of leg two.*

Stuart Bannatyne, Watch Captain
Age 30, New Zealand
Experience:
1993–94 *New Zealand Endeavour*
1997–98 *Silk Cut*

Stu Bettany, Bow
Age 29, New Zealand
Experience: 1997–98 *Innovation Kvaerner*

Richard Clarke, Helm/Trimmer
Age 32, Canada

Mark Christensen, Watch Captain
Age 31, New Zealand
Experience:
1993–94 *Winston*
1997–98 *EF Language*

Ray Davies, Helm/Trimmer
Age 29, New Zealand
Experience: 1997–98 *Merit Cup*

Dirk de Ridder, Trimmer
Age 28, The Netherlands
Experience: 1997–98 *Merit Cup*

Noel Drennan, Helm/Trimmer
 (legs two–five, and seven)
Age 40, Ireland

Jamie Gale, Mast
Age 29, New Zealand

Ross Halcrow, Trimmer
Age 34, New Zealand
Experience:
1989–90 *Fisher & Paykel*
1997–98 *Innovation Kvaerner* (one leg)

Tony Kolb, Bow
Age 25, Germany

Ian Moore, Navigator (legs one and six)
Age 30, Ireland

Ed Adams, Tactician (legs eight and nine)
Age 45, USA

News Corp

Jez Fanstone, Skipper
Age 35, United Kingdom
Experience: 1997–98 *Silk Cut*

Ross Field, Syndicate Head/Navigator (legs one–five)
Age 52, New Zealand
Experience:
1985–86 *NZI Enterprise*
1989–90 *Steinlager 2*
1993–94 *Yamaha*
1997–98 *America's Challenge*

Nick White, Navigator/Meteorology/Media
 (legs one, two, four, and six)
Age 33, New Zealand
Experience: 1993–94 *Yamaha*

Craig Smith, Helm
Age 34, New Zealand

Steve Cotton, Watch Leader (legs one–five)
Age 33, Australia
Experience:
1993–94 *Yamaha*
1997–98 *Toshiba*

Jeff Scott, Watch Leader (legs one–four)
Age 37, New Zealand
Experience:
1989–90 *Fisher & Paykel*
1993–94 *Yamaha*
1997–98 *Toshiba*

Alastair Pratt, Trimmer/Sail Coordinator
Age 31, Australia
Experience:
1993–94 *Brooksfield*
1997–98 *Innovation Kvaerner*

Jon Gundersen, Trimmer/Media (legs one–three)
Age 26, New Zealand

Damien Duke, Bow
Age 24, Australia

Justin Slattery, Bow/Medic/Rigger
Age 27, Ireland

Ian "Barney" Walker, Helm/Tactician
Age 38, Australia
Experience: 1997–98 *Innovation Kvaerner/Toshiba*

Peter Isler, Tactician/Navigator (legs three and nine)
Age 39, USA

Gordon MacGuire, Helm (leg two onward)
Age 46, Ireland
Experience:
1989–90 *Rothmans*
1993–94 *Winston*
1997–98 *Silk Cut*

*News Corp **heads toward Hobart on leg three.***

Joe Spooner, Trimmer (leg one only)
Age 27, New Zealand

Nigel King, Trimmer (legs four–eight)
Age 32, United Kingdom

Peter "Spike" Dorien, Trimmer (leg five onward)
Age 30, Australia

Matthew Humphries, Watch Leader (leg five onward)
Age 30, United Kingdom
Experience:
1989–90 *With Integrity*
1993–94 *Dolphin & Youth*
1997–98 *Swedish Match*

Stuart Childerley, Helm (legs six and seven)
Age 35, United Kingdom

Campbell Field, Navigator (legs seven and eight)
Age 31, New Zealand

Jeremy Robinson, Helm (leg eight only)
Age 35, United Kingdom

SEB

Gunnar "Gurra" Krantz, Skipper
Age 46, Sweden
Experience:
1989–90 *The Card*
1993–94 *Intrum Justitia*
1997–98 Skipper *Swedish Match*

David "Dingo" Rolfe, Helm/Trimmer
 (off leg three)
Age 32, New Zealand
Experience: 1997–98 *Swedish Match*

Gareth Cooke, Trimmer
Age 32, New Zealand

Glen John Kessels, Trimmer
Age 30, United Kingdom
Experience: 1993–94 *Dolphin & Youth*

Magnus Woxèn, Helm/Trimmer
Age 30, Sweden
Experience: 1997–98 *Swedish Match*

Marcel van Triest, Navigator
Age 37, The Netherlands
Experience:
1989–90 *Equity & Law II*
1993–94 *Intrum Justitia*
1997–98 *Innovation Kvaerner*

Matthew Humphries, Watch Captain (legs one–three)
Age 30, United Kingdom
Experience:
1989–90 *With Integrity*
1993–94 *Dolphin & Youth*
1997–98 *Swedish Match*

Rodney Ardern, Watch Captain
Age 31, New Zealand
Experience:
1993–94 *Tokio*
1997–98 *Swedish Match*

Tom Braidwood, Foredeck
Age 29, Australia

Tony Mutter, Watch Captain
Age 32, New Zealand
Experience: 1997–98 *Swedish Match*

Scott Beavis, Foredeck (legs one–five)
Age 21, New Zealand

Santiago Lange, Trimmer/Helm (leg one only)
Age 40, Argentina

Rodney Keenan, Trimmer (leg two only)
Age 28, New Zealand

Tony Rey, Trimmer (leg three only)
Age 34, USA
Experience:1997–98 *Chessie Racing*

*SEB **with the white cliffs of Dover in the background
bound for north sea and Göteborg.***

Sean Clarkson, Trimmer (leg three only)
Age 34, New Zealand
Experience:
1993–94 *New Zealand Endeavor*
1997–98 *Toshiba*

Pascal Bidegorry, Helm (leg four only)
Age 34, France

Anthony Merrington, Trimmer (legs four–eight)
Age 28, Australia

Jon Gundersen, Trimmer (leg five onward)
Age 26, New Zealand

Mark Reynolds, Tactician/Helm (leg six only)
Age 46, USA

Gavin Brady, Helm (legs seven and nine)
Age 29, USA/New Zealand
Experience: 1997–98 *Chessie Racing*

Steve Cotton, Watch Captain/Helm
    (legs eight and nine)
Age 33, Australia
Experience:
1993–94 *Yamaha*
1997–98 *Toshiba*

Tyco

Kevin Shoebridge, Skipper
Age 38, New Zealand
Experience:
1985–86 *Lion New Zealand*
1989–90 *Steinlager 2*
1993–94 *New Zealand Endeavour*
1997–98 *Merit Cup*

Steve Hayles, Navigator
Age 28, United Kingdom
Experience:
1993–94 *Dolphin and Youth*
1997–98 *Silk Cut*

Jim Close, Helmsman/Trimmer (legs one–four)
Age 33, Australia
Experience:
1989–90 *The Card*
1993–94 *Tokio*
1997–98 *Innovation Kvaerner*

Jan Dekker, Bow/Medic
Age 33, South Africa/France
Experience: 1997–98 *Silk Cut*

David Endean, Mast/Foredeck
Age 22, New Zealand

Brad Jackson, Watch Leader
Age 33, New Zealand
Experience:
1993–94 *New Zealand Endeavour*
1997–98 *Merit Cup*

Gerrard "Gerry" Mitchell, Helm/Trimmer
Age 31, United Kingdom
Experience:
1993–94 *Dolphin and Youth*
1997–98 *Silk Cut*

Tim Powell, Watch Leader
Age 30, United Kingdom
Experience:
1993–94 *Dolphin and Youth*
1997–98 *Silk Cut*

Guy Salter, Bow (off leg nine)
Age 29, United Kingdom

Rob Salthouse, Helm/Trimmer
Age 35, New Zealand

Jonathon Swain, Helm/Trimmer
Age 34, South Africa
Experience: 1997–98 *Chessie Racing*

Damion Foxall, Mast/Pit (off legs three and eight)
Age 32, Ireland

Richard Dodson, Mast/Pit (leg three only)
Age 42, New Zealand

Grant "Fuzz" Spanhake, Sail Maker
    (legs five, six, eight, and nine)
Age 42, New Zealand
Experience:
1985–86 *Lion New Zealand*
1989–90 *Fisher & Paykel*
1997–98 *Chessie Racing*

Richard Meacham, Sail Designer (leg seven only)
Age 25, New Zealand

Mike Quilter, Weather Strategy (leg eight only)
Age 48, New Zealand
Experience:
1989–90 *Steinlager 2*
1993–94 *New Zealand Endeavour*
1997–98 *Merit Cup*

Tyco at the Rangitoto Light House during leg four.

Crew List by Country

ARGENTINA
Santiago Lange ....SEB

AUSTRALIA
David Blanchfield ....djuice
Tom Braidwood ....SEB
Jim Close ....Tyco
Steve Cotton ....News Corp/SEB
Peter Dorien ....djuice/News Corp
Damien Duke.........................News Corp
Anthony Merrington ....SEB
Peter Merrington ....djuice
Chris Nicholson ....Amer Sports One
Anthony Nossiter ....djuice
Alastair Pratt...........................News Corp
Ian "Barney" Walker ....News Corp
Elizabeth Wardley ....Amer Sports Too
Emma Westmacott ......Amer Sports Too
Grant Wharington..........................djuice
Genevieve White..........Amer Sports Too

CANADA
Jeff Brock ....Amer Sports One
Richard Clarke ....illbruck

DENMARK
Stig Westergaard ....djuice

FRANCE
Jean-Yves Bernot...........................djuice
Pascal Bidegorry ....SEB
Christine Briand ....Amer Sports Too

Thomas Colville ....djuice
Herve Cunningham.........................djuice
Sidney Gavignet ....Assa Abloy
Herve Jan ....Assa Abloy
Jules Mazars ....Assa Abloy
Franck Proffit..................................djuice
Jacques Vincent ....djuice

GERMANY
Tony Kolb ....illbruck

IRELAND
Noel Drennan ....illbruck
Damion Foxall...................................Tyco
Gordon MacGuire ....News Corp
Ian Moore ....illbruck
Justin Slattery ....News Corp

ITALY
Claudio Celon ....Amer Sports One
Stefano Rizzi ....Amer Sports One

THE NETHERLANDS
Bouwe Bekking ....Amer Sports One
Carolijn Brouwer..........Amer Sports Too
Roy Heiner ....Assa Abloy
Willemien van Hoeve....Amer Sports Too
Dirk de Ridder ....illbruck
Marcel van Triest ....SEB
Wouter Verbraak ....djuice
Klaartje Zuiderbaan......Amer Sports Too

NEW ZEALAND
Phil Airey ....Amer Sports One
Joshua Alexander ....Assa Abloy
Rodney Arden ....SEB
Stuart Bannatyne ....illbruck
Scott Beavis ....SEB
Stu Bettany ....illbruck
Mark Christensen ....illbruck
Sean Clarkson.....................................SEB
Gareth Cooke.....................................SEB
Grant Dalton ....Amer Sports One
Ray Davies ....illbruck
Richard Dodson ....Tyco
David Endean ....Tyco
Sharon Ferris ....Amer Sports Too
Campbell Field......................News Corp
Ross Field ....News Corp
Jamie Gale ....illbruck
Jon Gundersen ....News Corp/SEB
Ross Halcrow ....illbruck
Keryn Henderson ....Amer Sports Too
Brad Jackson ....Tyco
Rodney Keenan ....SEB
Richard Mason ....Assa Abloy
Richard Meacham ....Tyco
Tony Mutter ....SEB
Mike Quilter ....Tyco
David Rolfe ....SEB
Rob Salthouse ....Tyco
Jeff Scott ....djuice/News Corp
Kevin Shoebridge ....Tyco
Craig Smith ....News Corp

Grant Spanhake...............................Tyco
Joe Spooner ....News Corp
Bridget Suckling ....Amer Sports Too
Nick White ....News Corp
Erle Williams ....djuice
Stu Wilson ....Assa Abloy

NORWAY
Knut Frostad ....djuice
Espen Guttormsen ....djuice
Christen Horn Johannessen ....djuice
Arve Roas ....djuice

SOUTH AFRICA
Jan Dekker.......................................Tyco
Mike Joubert ....Assa Abloy
Jonathon Swain ....Tyco

SPAIN
Guillermo Altadill..................Assa Abloy
Roberto Bermudez
de Castro..............................Assa Abloy
Pepe Ribes Rubio ....Amer Sports One
Juan Vila ....illbruck

SWEDEN
Anna Drougge..............Amer Sports Too
Gunnar Krantz ....SEB
Fredrik Loof ....Amer Sports One
Mikael Lundh ....djuice
Roger Nilson ....Amer Sports One
Klas Nylôf ....Assa Abloy

Magnus Olsson ....Assa Abloy
Jonas Wackenhuth.........................djuice
Magnus Woxén...............................SEB

UNITED KINGDOM

Joanna Burchell ....Amer Sports Too
Jason Carrington ....Assa Abloy
Stuart Childerley ....News Corp
Jez Fanstone ....News Corp
Eleanor Hay.................Amer Sports Too
Steve Hayles ....Tyco
Matthew Humphries ....SEB/News Corp
David Jarvis ....djuice
Glen John Kessels..............................SEB
Nigel King......................News Corp
Neal McDonald ....Assa Abloy
Miranda Merron ....Amer Sports Too
Gerrard Mitchell ....Tyco
Tim Powell ....Tyco
Emma Richards...........Amer Sports Too
Jeremy Robinson ....News Corp
Guy Salter ....Tyco
Abigail Seager ....Amer Sports Too

UNITED STATES

Ed Adams ....illbruck
Gavin Brady ....SEB
Paul Cayard ....Amer Sports One
Steve Gruver ....djuice
Mike Howard ....Assa Abloy
Terry Hutchinson ....djuice
Peter Isler ....News Corp
Keith Kilpatrick ....Amer Sports One
John Kostecki ....illbruck
Chris Larson ....:.....Assa Abloy
Lisa McDonald ....Amer Sports Too
Peter Pendleton ....Amer Sports One
Katie Pettibone ....Amer Sports Too
Melissa Purdy ....Amer Sports Too
Tony Rey ....SEB
Mark Reynolds ....SEB
Mark Rudiger ....Assa Abloy

Dee Smith ....Amer Sports One

Total Crew per Country

ARGENTINA 1
AUSTRALIA 16
CANADA 2
DENMARK 1
FRANCE 10
GERMANY 1
IRELAND 5
ITALY 2
THE NETHERLANDS 8
NEW ZEALAND 37
NORWAY 4
SOUTH AFRICA 3
SPAIN 4
SWEDEN 9
UNITED KINGDOM 18
USA...18
Total Crew Number **139**

Crew List Alphabetically

A

Ed Adams ....illbruck
Phil Airey ....Amer Sports One
Joshua Alexander ....Assa Abloy
Guillermo Altadill................Assa Abloy
Rodney Ardern ....SEB

B

Stuart Bannatyne ....illbruck
Scott Beavis ....SEB
Bouwe Bekking ....Amer Sports One
Roberto Bermudez
de Castro ....Assa Abloy
Jean-Yves Bernot................djuice
Stu Bettany......................illbruck
Pascal Bidegorry ....SEB
David Blanchfield ....djuice
Gavin Brady ....SEB
Tom Braidwood ....SEB

Christine Briand ....Amer Sports Too
Jeff Brock ....Amer Sports One
Carolijn Brouwer........Amer Sports Too
Joanna Burchell ....Amer Sports Too

C

Jason Carrington ....Assa Abloy
Paul Cayard ....Amer Sports One
Claudio Celon ....Amer Sports One
Richard Clarke ....illbruck
Stuart Childerley ....News Corp
Mark Christensen ....illbruck
Sean Clarkson ....SEB
Jim Close ....Tyco
Thomas Colville ....djuice
Gareth Cooke ....SEB
Steve Cotton ....News Corp/SEB
Herve Cunningham ....djuice

D

Grant Dalton ....Amer Sports One
Ray Davies ....illbruck
Jan Dekker ....Tyco
Richard Dodson ....Tyco
Peter Dorien ....djuice/News Corp
Noel Drennan.............................illbruck
Anna Drougge...........Amer Sports Too
Damien Duke ....News Corp

E

David Endean ....Tyco

F

Jez Fanstone ....News Corp
Sharon Ferris ....Amer Sports Too
Campbell Field.....................News Corp
Ross Field ....News Corp
Damion Foxall ....Tyco
Knut Frostad ....djuice

G

Jamie Gale ....illbruck
Sidney Gavignet ....Assa Abloy

Steve Gruver................................djuice
Jon Gundersen ....News Corp/SEB
Espen Guttormsen ....djuice

H

Ross Halcrow ....illbruck
Eleanor Hay ....Amer Sports Too
Steve Hayles ....Tyco
Roy Heiner ....Assa Abloy
Keryn Henderson ....Amer Sports Too
Willemien van Hoeve....Amer Sports Too
Mike Howard ....Assa Abloy
Matthew Humphries....SEB/News Corp
Terry Hutchinson ....djuice

I

Peter Isler ....News Corp

J

Brad Jackson ....Tyco
Herve Jan ....Assa Abloy
David Jarvis..................................djuice
Christen Horn Johannessen ....djuice
Mike Joubert.......................Assa Abloy

K

Rodney Keenan ....SEB
Glen John Kessels ....SEB
Keith Kilpatrick ....Amer Sports One
Nigel King ....News Corp
Tony Kolb................................illbruck
John Kostecki ....illbruck
Gunnar Krantz...............................SEB

L

Santiago Lange................................SEB
Chris Larson ....Assa Abloy
Fredrik Loof ....Amer Sports One
Mikael Lundh ....djuice

M

Gordon MacGuire ....News Corp
Richard Mason ....Assa Abloy

Jules Mazars ....Assa Abloy
Lisa McDonald ....Amer Sports Too
Neal McDonald ....Assa Abloy
Richard Meacham...........................Tyco
Miranda Merron ....Amer Sports Too
Anthony Merrington ....SEB
Peter Merrington...........................djuice
Gerrard Mitchell ....Tyco
Ian Moore.................................illbruck
Tony Mutter....................................SEB

N

Chris Nicholson ....Amer Sports One
Roger Nilson ....Amer Sports One
Anthony Nossiter ....djuice
Klas Nylôf.............................Assa Abloy

O

Magnus Olsson ....Assa Abloy

P

Peter Pendleton ....Amer Sports One
Katie Pettibone ....Amer Sports Too
Tim Powell ....Tyco
Alastair Pratt ....News Corp
Franck Proffit ....djuice
Melissa Purdy ....Amer Sports Too

Q

Mike Quilter ....Tyco

R

Tony Rey ....SEB
Mark Reynolds.................................SEB
Pepe Ribes Rubio ......Amer Sports One
Emma Richards..........Amer Sports Too
Dirk de Ridder ....illbruck
Stefano Rizzi ....Amer Sports One
Arve Roaas ....djuice
Jeremy Robinson ....News Corp
David Rolfe ....SEB
Mark Rudiger ....Assa Abloy

S

Guy Salter......................................Tyco
Rob Salthouse ....Tyco
Jeff Scott ....djuice/News Corp
Abigail Seager ....Amer Sports Too
Kevin Shoebridge ....Tyco
Justin Slattery......................News Corp
Craig Smith ....News Corp
Dee Smith ....Amer Sports One
Grant Spanhake ....Tyco
Joe Spooner ....News Corp
Bridget Suckling ....Amer Sports Too
Jonathon Swain ....Tyco

T

Marcel van Triest ....SEB

V

Wouter Verbraak...........................djuice
Juan Vila......................................illbruck
Jacques Vincent ....djuice

W

Jonas Wackenhuth ....djuice
Ian "Barney" Walker ....News Corp
Elizabeth Wardley ......Amer Sports Too
Stig Westergaard ....djuice
Emma Westmacott ....Amer Sports Too
Grant Wharington.......................djuice
Genevieve White........Amer Sports Too
Nick White..........................News Corp
Erle Williams.................................djuice
Stu Wilson ....Assa Abloy
Magnus Woxèn ....SEB

Z

Klaartje Zuiderbaan ......Amer Sports Too

The Volvo fleet in the harbor in Auckland.

Volvo Event Management

Big sporting events, ranging from the Olympics to world championships in every sport, capture the imagination of the public. But what is rarely understood is the thorough management required to run such world-class events. Ocean racing in particular presents a complex mosaic of issues including fairness, safety, funding, multiple venues, and coordinating an endless list of tasks. The Volvo Ocean Race is unique because the sponsoring company actually owns the event.

Following the 1997–98 Whitbread Race, Volvo acted swiftly to name the host ports, recruit a competitive fleet, develop a comprehensive media plan, enlist complimentary event sponsors, and keep safety paramount. A mission statement was adopted:

"To ensure that the Volvo Ocean Race remains the Premier Ocean Race and to use Volvo's world-wide communication experience to Attract, Excite, and Inspire a global audience to make the Volvo Ocean Race an effective marketing and communication tool for all the stakeholders involved."

Volvo acquired a two-story building for its home in Whiteley, Fareham, about 15 miles north of Southampton, England. The building was appropriately named Ocean House.

Over the 3-year buildup, the permanent staff grew from 8 to 32 people. Experts in a variety of fields were hired to bring additional skills.

The format and rules for the race were written by the Race Committee, led by Chairman Ian Bailey-Willmot, the former Chief Executive of the Whitbread Round The World Race. This group met 21 times over a 3-year period. The decisions made by the Race Committee set the standard for ocean racing worldwide.

Once the Volvo Ocean Race was under way the race operations became the nerve center of all information. Race Officials were in each port working closely with the syndicates and local race committees. Back at Ocean House, the staff kept track of the fleet. Teams worked on 12-hour shifts and were available for all emergency communications.

After 3 years of preparation, the staff had every port ready to receive the fleet. Each stopover had its own personality. The logistics included a land and waterside base for the yachts, repair facilities, sail loft, and the coordination of numerous events hosted by local organizers. Coordinating the task was huge.

Over three million unique visitors spent time on the volvooceanrace.org web site. For the first time the round-the-world race featured regular radio reports. Volvo's staff included on-site press officers and two writers back at Ocean House.

Granada Sport produced the world TV feed and news pool images. Granada's 38 shows were customized for 11 territories throughout the world. The still photography archive was massive with over 10,000 images.

The combined budgets of the Volvo Ocean Race, the 10 ports of call, the seven syndicates, and the primary media exceeded $250 million (US). Every stakeholder came away from the Volvo Ocean Race 2001–2002 a winner.

Volvo Ocean Race Headquarters Operations Room, manned 24 hours a day while the fleet was at sea.

Race Committee

Helge Alten	Gary Jobson
Ian Bailey-Willmot	Sonia Mayes
Michael Broughton	Magnus Olsson
Joao Cabecadas	Mel Pyatt
Pascal Conq	Tim Spalding
Chris Cooney	Mike Urwin
E. Alan Green	John Warren
Audy Hindley	Michael Woods
Rob Humphreys	

Race Organization (Alphabetical)

Helge Alten
Chief Executive

Kina Alten
Traveling Accountant

Patrick Anderson
Picture Desk Manager

Peter Ansell
Logistics Manager

Ian Bailey-Willmot
Chairman of the Race Commitee

Marion Brennan
Project Manager—Internet

John Capon
Financial Controller

Chris Cooney
Director of Logistics

Roger Court
IT Technician

Allison Crook
PA to Chief Executive

Peter Dakin
Production Manager - Internet

Mark Dwyer
Technical Project Manager

Andrew Ferguson
IT Technician

Lizzie Green
Race Press Officer

Debbie Hadwen
Duty Officer

Darren Hampton
System Administrator

Andreas Hanakamp
Press Officer UK

Rachel Healey
Media Assistant

Andy Hindley
Yacht Equipment and Race Manager

Mark Howell
Media Director

Sandry Koo
Events Manager

Anders Lofgren
Commercial Director

Timo Malinen
Race Chiropractor

Patrick Marshall
Television Consultant

Sonia Mayes
Rules Advisor

Anne Prees
Duty Officer

Emily Robertson
Producer—Internet

Peter Rusch
Media Centre Manager

Anna Shattky
Assistant Events Manager

Louise Spackman
Assistant Events

Johnny Stokes
Assistant Events

Guy Swindells
Radio Producer

Mike Stickney
Media and Marketing Consultant

Annika Tomlinson
Traveling Office Co-ordinator

Rick Tomlinson
Official Photographer

Faye Walker
General Secretary

David Wise
Race Operations Room Manager

Lisa Woods
Duty Officer

Michael Woods
Director of Race Operations

Above: Volvo Ocean Race Village before the Prize Giving Ceremony in Göteborg, Sweden.

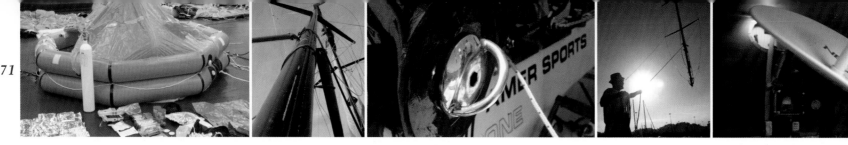

Glossary of Terms

Aft: Toward the rear of the yacht.

Apparent Wind: The perceived wind direction of a moving yacht. When the yacht goes faster, the perceived wind direction moves forward, just as the wind always seems to hit a car only from head-on as it drives at high speeds.

Backstay: A mast support that runs from the top of the mast to the stern of the yacht; it may be adjustable in order to bend the mast backward or to increase tension on the forestay.

Ballast: Weight in the keel of a boat to add stability (righting moment). The ballast on a V.O.60 includes water, which can be pumped into tanks on each side of the boat. Can equate to up to an extra 30 people sitting on the windward side.

Beam: A boat's greatest width.

Beating: Sailing (or pointing) at an angle into the wind or upwind. Since sailboats cannot sail directly into the wind, "beating" is the closest course to the wind they can sail.

Berth: a) The place where you put the boat on a dock; b) Bunk or sleeping quarters

Bilge: The lowest part of a boat's hull.

Block: A deck or track-mounted pulley device through which ropes such as jib and genoa sheets are strung.

Boom: A spar to which a sail's lower edge or "foot" is attached. The boom is attached to the mast at the gooseneck.

Bosun's Chair: A seat, usually made of canvas, used to hoist a person up the mast.

Bow: The front of the boat.

Bowman: The crew member in charge of sail changes and keeping a lookout on the bow at the start.

Broach: When a keelboat sailing on a run capsizes from a strong puff of wind or gets knocked down by a wave. Also called a **Knockdown** or a **Wipeout**.

Bulb: The lead-torpedo shape on the bottom of the keel.

Bulkhead: A partition to strengthen the frame of a yacht.

Buoy: A marker used for navigation, mooring, or racing around.

Cam Cleat: A mechanical cleat used to hold a line automatically. It uses two spring-loaded cams (teeth) that come together to clamp the line, which is placed between them.

Capsize: To turn upside down.

Chainplates: The metal or composite attachments for shrouds and stays. Part of the hull, connecting the hull with the rigg.

Chute: A spinnaker.

Cleat: A fitting, typically with projecting ends, that holds a line against the tension from the sails, rigging, or mooring.

Clew: The lower corner of a mainsail, jib, or genoa and either lower corner of a spinnaker attached to the sheet.

Cockpit: A recessed area in the deck in which the crew works.

Code 0: A tight luff, upwind spinnaker developed by *EF Language* during the 1997–98 Whitbread race, also called "the Whomper."

Compass: An instrument that uses the earth's magnetic field to point to the direction of the magnetic North Pole; used by navigators to determine the direction a yacht is heading and to set a course.

Course: The direction a yacht is sailing.

Crew: The team of sailors that sails the yacht.

Dacron: A white woven sailcloth made of a polyester fiber. Brand name by DuPont.

Dead downwind: Sailing straight with the wind.

Deck: Horizontal surface or platform of a yacht.

Delaminating: A failure of the bond between either of the hull's outer and inner skins, and the "sandwich" spacing material in between—allowing either of the two outer layers to become unstuck from the core.

Dismast: To lose, through breakage, part or all of the mast.

Doldrums: An area between the weather systems of the Northern and Southern Hemispheres characterized by frustrating light winds, major shifts in wind direction, and sudden violent squalls.

Downwind: The point of sail when the wind blows from aft of the yacht's beam.

EPIRB: Emergency Position Indicating Radio Beacon. There are two types of beacon. One is a transmitter that all commercial vessels are required to have on board. Pleasure crafts are recommended to carry one. The second type is a personal EPIRB that sailors wear on themselves, either as a watch, within their clothing, or around their neck so they can be located should they be washed overboard.

Equator: Line of latitude at 0 degrees—equal distance from both poles.

Foot: The bottom edge of a sail.

Foredeck: The area of a yacht's deck that is in front of the mast; also a crew position aboard a racing yacht.

Foresail: Any sail used between the mast and the forestay.

Forestay: A mast support that runs from the top of the mast, or near the top of the mast, to the bow.

Fractional Rig: A rig where the headstay does not go to the top of the mast.

Furious Fifties: An area between 50 degrees and 60 degrees latitude noted for very strong winds and huge seas.

Galley: Kitchen.

Gennaker: A cross between a genoa and a spinnaker, a foresail used for reaching.

Genoa: A large foresail that overlaps the shroud base used for sailing upwind; also called a "genny."

GPS: Global Positioning System. Satellite navigation, which gives yachts exact latitude and longitude position. The update rate is one second.

Guy: A rope used to adjust the position of a spinnaker pole.

Gybe: See **Jibe**

Gooseneck: The mechanical device connecting the boom and the mast.

Halyard: A line used to hoist and hold up a sail.

Head: a) Toilet/Basin/Shower b) The top corner of a sail that is connected to the halyard.

Header: A wind shift during which the wind enters the boat more forward.

Headsail: A sail flown between the mast and the bow of the yacht.

Helm: The steering station of a yacht; the tiller or wheel by which the rudder is controlled.

Helmsman: The crewmember who steers the yacht; usually also the skipper; also called the "driver."

Hounds: The attachment points for the shrouds up the mast.

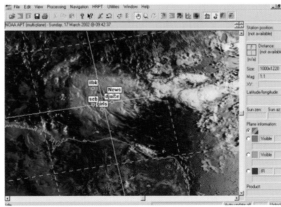
A screen grab showing the position of the fleet using GPS.

Hull: The body of a yacht.

Inmarsat-C: A digital store and forward messaging service, using satellites for transmission.

Jib: A foresail that fits in between the forestay and the mast.

Jibe: The process of turning the yacht so that the stern turns through the wind, thereby changing the side of the yacht on which the sails are carried (opposite of tacking); also spelled **gybe**.

Jury-rig: Emergency rigging with available gear, usually due to a broken mast.

Keel: A ballasted appendage projecting below the boat that keeps it from capsizing, which also supplies the hydrodynamic lateral force that enables the boat to sail upwind.

Kevlar: Man-made, yellow/brown aramid fiber that is used to make sails or composites for building hulls. In sails it retains its shape better and is lighter than Dacron, but is more expensive. Kevlar is the brand name from DuPont and is also used in bullet-proof jackets. It loses its good properties when exposed to the sun for extended periods of time.

Kite: A spinnaker

Knockdown: See **Broach**.

Knot: a) One nautical mile per hour. b) Connection of lines.

Latitude: Angular distance north or south of the equator; measured from 0 to 90 degrees north or south.

Layline: An imaginary line projecting at an angle corresponding to the wind direction from either side of a racecourse marker buoy that defines the optimum sailing angle for a yacht to fetch the mark or the finish line. When a yacht reaches this point, it is said to be "on the layline." Going beyond the layline means the yacht is sailing a greater distance to reach the mark or finish line.

Leech: The trailing edge of a sail.

Leeward: Away from the wind. A leeward yacht is one that has another yacht between it and the wind (opposite of windward).

Life Raft: An inflatable craft into which the crew of a yacht transfers if the yacht intends to sink.

Lifelines: Cables that are held in place by stanchions and go around the boat to prevent people falling overboard. A "fence" around the boat on the edge of the deck.

Lift: A wind shift during which the wind enters the boat from further back. It allows the helmsman to head up or alter course to windward, or the crew to ease sheets.

Lines: A nautical term for ropes.

Longitude: Angular distance east or west of the Greenwich Meridian, measured from 0 to 180 degrees east or west.

Luff: a) To change course toward the wind. b) The leading edge of a sail.

Mainsheet Trimmer: A device that controls the position and shape of the mainsail, the large triangular sail behind the mast.

Mast: The vertical spar that holds up the sails.

Mastman: The crew member who works the lines on the mast when hoisting sails and who assists the bowman with the work on the foredeck.

Masthead Rig: A rigging scheme in which the forestay is attached near the top of the mast. See **Fractional Rig**.

Match Racing: A racing format where only two yachts compete at a time, like a boxing match, as opposed to "fleet racing" where more yachts sail at once.

Maxi: A boat designed to the maximum rating allowed under the International Offshore Rule, or more recently, the international measurement system.

Nautical Mile: The unit of geographical distance used on "salt-water" charts. 1 nautical mile corresponds exactly to 1 minute of angular distance on the meridian (adjacent left and right side of a sea chart). This facilitates navigation as it avoids a complicated conversion from angle to distance. 1 nautical mile equals 1,852 kilometers. 60 minutes equal 1 degree.

Navigator: The crew member who monitors the yacht's location and progress relative to the race course and the other yachts.

Off the Wind: Sailing away from the wind, also downwind, reaching, or running.

Peeling: Changing from one spinnaker to another.

Pitch-poling: Putting the bow into a wave and cartwheeling forward.

Pitman: Crew member who controls the halyards and mast winches and assists the mastman.

Pole: The spinnaker pole.

Port: Nautical term for the left side of a yacht when facing forward.

Port Tack: Sailing with the wind blowing onto the port side and the mainsail on the starboard side.

Reaching: All angles against the wind that are not beating or dead downwind. A close reach has the wind forward of abeam; a beam reach is when the wind is perpendicular to the boat; and a broad reach is when the wind is aft of abeam.

Rig: The general term used to describe a yacht's mast and sail combination.

Rigging: The wires, lines, halyards, and other items used to attach the sails and the spars to the boat. The lines that do not have to be adjusted often are known as standing rigging. The lines that are adjusted to raise, lower, and trim the sails are known as running rigging.

Roaring Forties: The area between 40 degrees and 50 degrees latitude noted for strong winds and large seas.

Running: Dead downwind.

Sat-phone: A satellite telephone. Unlike cellular phones that rely on networks of local antennae, sat-phones send and receive their signals directly to and from orbiting satellites. Though significantly more expensive than cellular phones, with calls costing from $4 to $9 a minute, sat-phones can operate from almost anywhere on earth. Each of the V.O.60 yachts is equipped with one.

The mast and rigging on SEB.

Screaming Sixties: The area between 60 degrees and 70 degrees latitude noted for exceptionally strong wind, huge seas, and frequent icebergs.

Sheet: A line that controls sails and adjusts their angle of attack and their trailing edge.

Shroud: A cable or rod that supports the mast side-wise. Shrouds run from the chainplates at deck level on the port and starboard side, to the hounds just below the top of the mast.

Sked: A position report issued every 6 hours.

Skipper: The person in charge of a vessel.

Southern Ocean: The ocean surrounding the Antarctic continent. The largest uninterrupted water on earth with the most dynamic weather systems, the highest waves, and the strongest winds (apart from tropical storms).

Spinnaker: A large ballooning sail that is flown in front of the yacht when the wind comes from aft of abeam. Spinnakers are used when running or reaching, sailing downwind. Also called **Kite** or **Chute**. The head is pulled to the top of the mast, using the halyard; the tack is at the spinnaker pole, projecting it away from the yacht; and the clew is connected to the sheet, trimming the sail.

Spinnaker Pole: A pole that is attached to the lower front of the mast to hold one corner of a spinnaker out from the yacht. On high-performance yachts, spinnaker poles are usually made of strong but lightweight carbon fiber composite material. When a spinnaker is not being flown, the pole is tethered to the deck.

Squall: The sudden, short-term burst of wind with passing clouds. May be accompanied by rain.

Stanchions: Vertical poles that stand on the outer edge of the deck to hold the lifelines.

Standing Rigging: The non-moving rods and lines that support the mast and sails.

Starboard: Nautical term for the right half of the yacht when facing forward.

Starboard Tack: Sailing with the wind blowing onto the starboard side, and the mainsail on the port side.

Staysail: A small sail flown between the mast and the inner forestay.

Stay: A rod or wire that supports the mast in a fore/aft position.

Stern: The rear of the boat.

Tack: a) The process of turning the bow of the yacht through the wind and changing the sides of the sails. b) The lower corner of a sail that is attached to the yacht.

Working the foredeck was easy in smooth water. The spinnaker and spinnaker pole are clearly shown.

Tiller: Traditionally the piece of wood the helmsman holds to control the rudder. Nowadays it can be made of aluminium, titanium, or a composite material in order to save weight.

Top: The high end of the mast.

Trade Wind: Northeast and southeast winds in the Atlantic blowing continually toward the equator. Named after the traditional trading ships, which sailed a course using these winds to their advantage.

Transom: The flat rear end of a boat, the upper part of which tends to lean forward on modern racers.

Trim: To adjust the sail to make it the right shape and angle to the wind.

Trysail: A triangular loose-footed sail fitted aft of the mast, often used to replace the mainsail in heavy weather.

Upwind: Sailing against the wind at an angle a certain yacht can achieve.

Velocity Made Good (VMG): The speed of a yacht relative to the waypoint it wants to reach, or toward or away from the wind.

Watches: Teams within which the crew operates, taking turns to work, sleep and eat.

Watch Leader/Captain: The person in charge of a watch.

Watertight Hatch: Watertight doors. In the event of a hull breach, the hatches can be closed to seal off compartments on the affected portion of the boat.

Waypoint: A specific location as defined by GPS, the Global Positioning System.

Winch: A device used to give a mechanical advantage when hauling on the lines.

Winch Pedestal: An upright winch drive mechanism with two handles to increase purchasing power.

Windward: Against the wind.

Wipeout: See **Broach**.

The fleet of V.O.60s at the start of leg four from Auckland to Rio de Janeiro.

Photo Credits

Rick Tomlinson: ii, vii, 4, 8, 9, 11, 12, 13, 15, 16, 17, 19, 20, 21, 24, 27, 28, 29, 30, 31, 32, 33, 34, 37, 38, 39, 44, 48, 49, 50, 52, 53, 56, 57, 59, 60, 61, 66, 69, 70, 72, 73, 74, 75, 76, 77, 78, 80, 81, 83, 84, 88, 89, 90, 91, 92, 94, 96, 97, 99, 100, 123, 126, 129, 130, 131, 135, 137, 142, 143, 158, 159, 160, 162, 164, 169, 170, 175, 176, back cover

Daniel Forster: front cover, i, 20, 21, 55, 56, 73, 163

Stephen Munday/Allsport: iv, 145

Mike Hewitt/Allsport: v

Roger Lean-Bercoe: vi, 133

Terry Murphy: vii, 159

Bob Grieser: 1

Jon Nash: 3, 38, 60, 79, 96, 99, 166, 171, 175

Oskar Kilhborg: 4, 7, 34, 35, 36, 41, 78, 93, 155, 166, 169, 171, 173, 174

Carlo Borlenghi: iii, 5, 23, 24, 25, 28, 52, 67, 71, 78, 157, 160, 165, 168, 171, 172

Patrick Anderson: 5, 38, 169, 171

Richard Mason: 12, 13, 14, 94, 160, 161

Ray Davies: 20, 22, 44, 68, 72, 75, 85

Guido Cantini: 24, 26, 86, 88, 90, 92, 96, 98, 160, 161, 169

Peter Bentley: 24, 45

Damien Duke: 30, 72, 87

Nick White: 30, 66

Richard Langdon: 30, 32, 50, 82, 95, 96, 97, 169

Magnus Woxen: 34, 35, 51, 52, 58, 60, 63, 84, 90

Andrew Ferguson: 34

Jens Fischer: 38, 39, 66, 90, 93

Thierry Martinez: 64

Warren Douglas: 72

Daniel Duke: 82

RJ Harris: 87

PPL: 101, 105, 107, 111, 116, 117, 122, 126, 129, 131, 135, 137, 138, 139, 140, 141, 144

Skip Novak: 103, 132, 133

PPL/Bob Fisher: 105, 109, 110, 111, 113, 117, 127, 129, 136, 141

PPL/Alistair Black: 108, 114, 115

PPL/David Alan Williams: 111

PPL/Robin Knox-Johnston: 111

PPL/Barry Pickthall: 111, 112, 114, 123, 124, 128

PPL/Onne Van der Wal: 117, 118, 119, 120, 121

PPL/Julian Fuller: 117, 125

PPL/Krall: 123

PPL/Jamie Lawson-Johnston: 137, 143

PPL/Mark Pepper: 137

PPL/Thomas Lundberg: 140

Allsport: 145, 146, 147, 148, 149, 150, 151, 152, 153, 154

Klaarbe Zuiderbaan: 166, 171

Guy Salter: 166

April 28—Restart for leg seven from Annapolis to La Rochelle.

Bibliography

Theirs is the Glory. Chay Blyth. London: Hodder and Stroughton, 1974.

Blake's Odyssey. Peter Blake and Alan Sefton. Auckland: Hodder and Stoughton, 1982.

The Greatest Race. Bob Fisher. Robertsbridge Limited of London, 1986.

One Watch At A Time. Skip Novak. New York: W.W. Norton & Company, 1988.

Fazisi. Skip Novak. London: Sidgwick and Jackson Ltd., 1990.

Whitbread Round The World 1973–1993. Peter Johnson. Southampton: Whitbread PLC, 1992.

Faster and Faster. Bob Fisher and Barry Pickthall. London: Adlard Coles Nautical, 1994.

Endeavour Winning the Whitbread. Grant Dalton and Glen Sowry. New Zealand: Hodder Headline, 1994.

Reaching Beyond: The Ultimate Ocean Race. United Kingdom: Grenville Books, The Book People Ltd., 1994.

Whitbread Round the World Race. Knut Frostad. Oslo: Grøndahl og Dreyers Forlag AS, 1998.

Risk to Gain. Rick Tomlinson, Mark Chisnell, and Max Ström. Stockholm: Bokförlaget DN, 1998.

Chessie Racing. George J. Collins and Kathy Alexander. Baltimore: The Johns Hopkins Press, 2001.

E-Credit: The Volvo Ocean Race Official History web site, 2001.

Crowds welcome the Volvo fleet to Kiel at the end of leg nine.

Acknowledgements

A book of this magnitude takes many people working together to publish. I would like to thank the following people:

My trusted assistant Kathy Thompson, for her tireless effort in Annapolis.

Kippy Requardt, who provided extensive research for the history and syndicate chapters.

Roger Vaughan, the writer of our ESPN series, who was extremely helpful providing information in the leg chapters.

I am grateful to Helge Alten, Skip Novak, and Paul Cayard for their insightful words.

I would like to thank Susan Kahan, of Nomad Press, who edited all my written material. Anna Typrowicz and Kristi Jobson for proofreading.

From the Volvo Ocean Race office, Lizzie Green worked with us from the beginning of the project to maintain the highest standards.

It has been a pleasure working with Alex Kahan, President of Nomad Press, who understands the big picture in promoting the sport of sailing.

Many thanks to designer Jeff McAllister, who pulled all the elements together to create a visually stunning book, Rachel Benoit for her behind-the-scenes efforts to get the book to press, and everyone else at Nomad Press who contributed to the book's success.

To Anders Lofgren who managed the commercial side of the project for the Volvo Ocean Race.

There is a saying that a picture is worth a thousand words; thanks to Rick Tomlinson and the other photographers for their beautiful work. The pictures literally jump off the page.

—Gary Jobson